Brighton's

People, place, culture

> 'Brighton has a particular spirit of place that comes from its people and its history. People come here to change, to experience something different, whether they move here, or whether they're just visiting for the weekend.'
>
> JANE MCMORROW, BRIGHTON FESTIVAL PROGRAMMER, 2001-2008[1]

1 J.M. Woodham, N. Butler, R. Ely, L. Aggiss, I. Smith, S. Fanshawe, S. Thomas, et al., *ZAP: Twenty-Five Years of Innovation* (Brighton: QueenSpark Books, 2007).

Acknowledgements

Published by QueenSpark Books, a charity which, since 1972, has helped the people of Brighton & Hove to tell their stories.

QueenSpark Books gratefully acknowledges the financial assistance of The National Lottery Heritage Fund, which made possible the Archives Alive project, and Brighton & Hove City Council and the University of Brighton for their ongoing support. With gratitude to all the volunteers and participants in Archives Alive.

Brighton's Alternative Spaces – People, place, culture

First published in Great Britain in 2019 by QueenSpark Books, Brighton, UK.

A catalogue record for this book is available from the British Library

ISBN 978-1-9996699-2-8

Designer Chris Callard www.beachstone.co.uk

Managing Editor John Riches

Developmental Editors Kevin Bacon (Photographs), Evlynn Sharp (Text)

Editors Gill Ditch, Hannah Smith and Siobhán Laroche

Photo Editors Ali Ghanimi, Daren Kay, Kavitha Ravikumar

Image archives James Gray Collection, QueenSpark Books, Regency Society, Royal Pavilion and Museums, Brighton & Hove

Printed by One Digital, Woodingdean www.one-digital.com

QueenSpark Books
admin@queensparkbooks.org.uk
Web www.queensparkbooks.org.uk

Registered Charity Number 1172938 Company Number 02404473

Foreword

Brighton's Alternative Spaces is a celebration of Brighton's alternative culture and the spaces across the city, which provide platforms and homes for creativity and innovation. As the writers and editors of this book, we wanted to explore how Brighton has earned its reputation and forged its identity as a haven for alternative culture.

Cultural spaces and places offer people a space and community where they feel they belong, and can truly express their individuality and creativity. In this book, we look at some of the spaces and individuals, both past and present, that make Brighton loved by so many for its unique, open-minded spirit and thriving cultural scene.

The chapters can stand alone – but recurring themes and characters that appear across the book mean chapters expand upon each other, too. *Brighton's Alternative Spaces* also features a guest chapter on alternative politics, kindly provided by Lisa Redlinski and Davy Jones.

Gill Ditch, Hannah Smith and Siobhán Laroche
Editors – *Brighton's Alternative Spaces*

July 2019

Burning the Clocks.
Procession through the
streets of Brighton, 2018
by Barry Pitman.

Contents

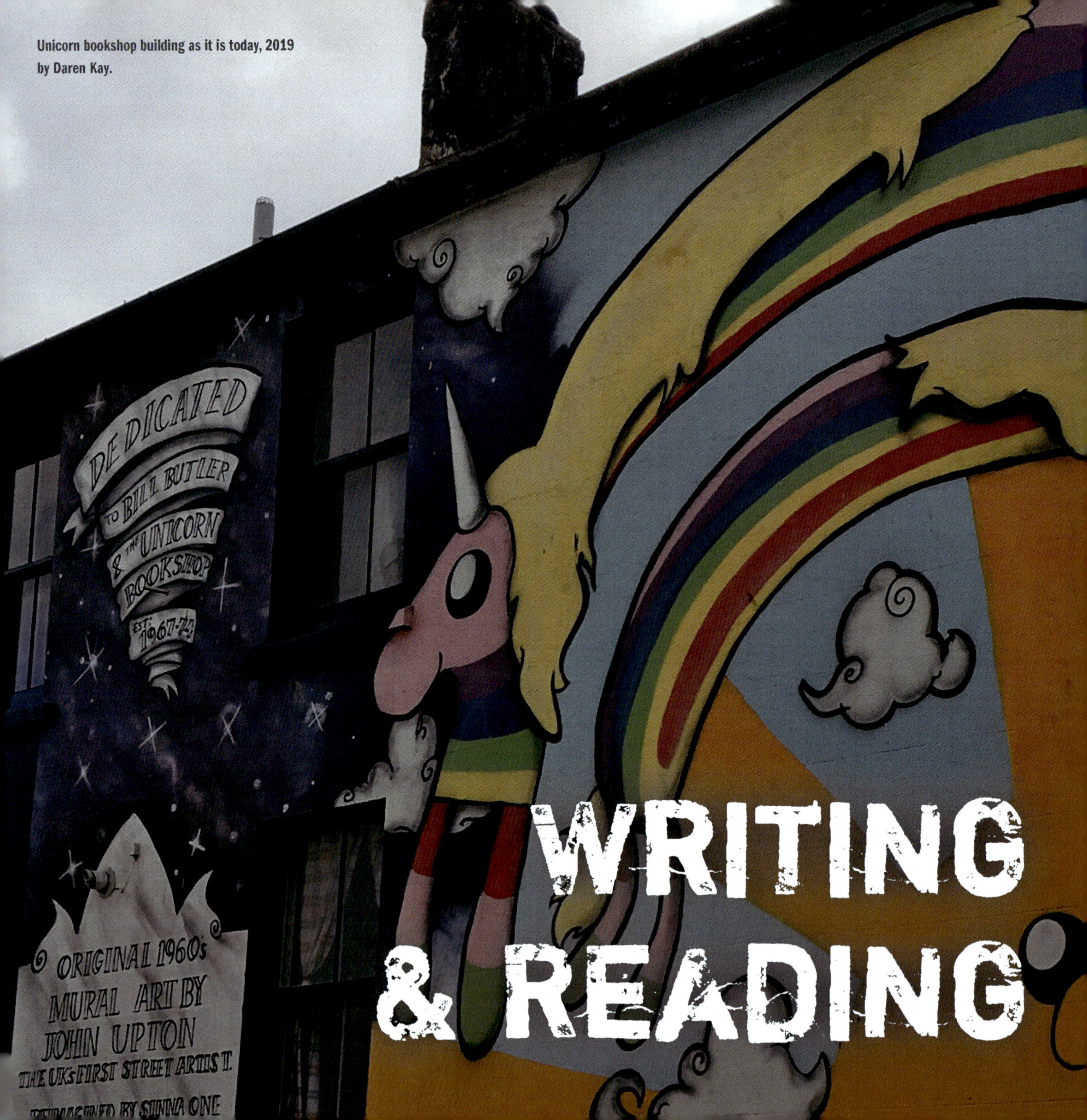

Unicorn bookshop building as it is today, 2019 by Daren Kay.

QueenSpark Origins

BORN FROM A GRASSROOTS CAMPAIGN IN 1972, community publisher QueenSpark Books has been instrumental in providing a platform for the expression of alternative local voices and stories. Their vision is clear and inclusive: "to inspire and involve residents of Brighton & Hove – in particular, people who are seldom heard – to share and preserve their stories in an artful and accessible way […]."[1]

This devotion to capturing social history is illustrated in over 110 books. QueenSpark fully embraces efforts to publish unconventional narratives from residents of all classes, genders, races and life experiences. Initially formed by a collective of local residents who wanted the 1824 Royal Spa in Queen's Park to be converted to a nursery school instead of the proposed casino, QueenSpark began as a widely circulated street newspaper that supplied information about the campaign. This tradition of group authorship developed into more detailed publications, varying from short autobiographical books to researched collations of social history shaped by volunteer contributors.

QueenSpark's willingness to give traditionally neglected citizens a public voice also led to the running of a number of local writing groups that drew together local residents who felt their voices and stories were at risk of being marginalized. Their collective work was subsequently published as collections of short stories and poetry by the cooperative.

These compilations included *Writers Reign* (1991), a grouping of stories "produced democratically by a number of people of differing ages and backgrounds",[2] and *Tales from the Sanctuary* (1995) that consisted of readings performed at Hove's Sanctuary Café. Contributor to *Writers Reign* Tom Woodin commends QueenSpark's integral role in carving out an alternative space through which non-discriminatory writing opportunities could be explored: "QueenSpark encourages local people to create and express their own culture, something hidden in our age of 'mass culture'."[3] For example, a stroke survivors' group was set up by two QueenSpark authors who had experienced life-altering strokes themselves and wanted to provide an alternative space for those with similar experiences to meet and encourage one another.

Stroke Survivors' Groups

In the 1990s, QueenSpark's Nick Osmond and stroke rehabilitation specialist Sister Jan Nowak ran weekly writing workshops with local stroke survivors to produce a detailed account of the challenges and victories of stroke recovery. The regular writing practice itself was also a key aspect of the process of rehabilitation as it allowed the survivors to "[...] share their experiences in a mutually beneficial and supportive way."[4] These community gatherings and literary experimentation resulted in QueenSpark's 1992 publication of *Life After Stroke*: "a compilation of compelling and courageous stories that proved there is indeed a life after suffering a stroke."[5]

Women's Writing Groups

QueenSpark Books' most popular and renowned writing groups proved to be those run for local women by local women. These weekly classes provided safe and non-judgmental spaces of free expression in which participants (regardless of social class) could engage in creative writing and critique, editing and performing their own and others' work.

Tillie Olsen writes in *Stories from the Nights at the Round Table* (see *Silences*[6]): "By the most generous estimate, simply the percentage of fiction of all manner and kind published, men are three quarters of the writing race; in the more selective and indicative estimates, they are 88% to 98%."[7] Yet at these regular sessions, local women were encouraged to explore and develop their own personal and literary voices evident in publications entitled *QueenSpark Women Writers*, *Writers Reign* and *From Circle to Spiral*.

Bright and early on a Tuesday morning in March 1984, a handful of budding female writers found themselves hanging outside an unsuspecting terraced house on 12 Hanover Crescent. On entering they were greeted by Jean and Maureen, the group convenors, and the group quickly "ascended to the first floor and entered a rather pleasant airy room at the front of the house."[8] This was to be one of the very first meetings of the QueenSpark Women Writers. Group Leader Maureen Ivermee recalls starting the group:

> ' In my work as an adult education teacher and working with local writers for QueenSpark, I met women who wanted to write, or who were already writing, but were put off by 'creative writing' classes, where accepted views about good literature seemed to be unquestioned. They did not feel their work belonged. The opposition of men, or even their amused tolerance, was another hindrance to writing. ' [9]

The groups became increasingly popular and attended by a wide variety of women whose age range spanned 40+ years. The alternative space that the QueenSpark writing groups provided proved to be the perfect setting for these women to vocalise and preserve their own fictional and autobiographical stories. This receptive environment also encouraged the formation of a tight-knit female community through which members such as 30-year-old Gina Jupp could "understand" themselves and no longer feel "alone and unusual."[10] Attendee Pepper Moth reflects on the supportive atmosphere the writing groups provided: "When I joined the group with all their understanding and kindness I suddenly found all the approval I needed."[11]

QueenSpark Women Writers was consequently published later that year, chock full of different styles and genres of storytelling composed during Maureen and Jean's weekly sessions. Contributor Sadie Abbiss points out that the book was not simply a finished product, but "part of [the group's] process of becoming writers, of seeing [themselves] as writers."[12] Another similar feminist-influenced anthology *Paper on the Wind* was also produced and published in 1984, consisting of a variety of poetry and prose from other female QueenSpark writing groups:

> For all of us it was important to take the first public step with other women, to be taken seriously without the kinds of criticism which destroy new and fragile confidence. We want to work hard at our writing, and make it better without feeling put down by other people's standards. SADIE ABBISS[13]

Alternative Writing Legacy

The legacy of alternative writing spaces continues to this day in Brighton and Hove with regular meet ups run by charities and local residents. Those interested in participating themselves or encouraging their partners, friends, or children to try story writing in an encouraging environment need look no further than Little Green Pig, New Writing South, Phoenix Writers, and groups facilitated and run by local libraries.

The Alternative Brighton Book Trade

In a location that so freely supported the expression and publication of alternative voices, it comes as no surprise that Brighton had a reputation for its plethora of radical and unconventional bookshops. In *Bookends,* John Shire pinpoints the earliest bookseller in the city as being a Mr Baker from Tunbridge Wells who set up shop in 1760 by the Steine.[14] Shire emphasises the popularity of local book businesses, with the early 19th century welcoming 103 booksellers to the city and "Meeting House Lane [seeing] twenty-nine booksellers come and go."[15] The latter half of the 20th century was when the alternative bookshop scene truly flourished in Brighton, with locals and tourists alike swarming to unique and novelty shops such as Public House Book Shop, Unicorn Book Shop, Solstice, Symposium, Avalon Books, Odd Volume and Bioscope. These stores were dotted all around the city and quickly became cultural hubs for loyal local customers. Functioning as more than simply bookshops, these buildings became social epicentres that supported their customers' exploration of the unconventional in an unprejudiced space. Their unusual and often radical book selections were mirrored in the idiosyncratic characters that owned and frequented the shops. Shire highlights the alternative community spirit that they harnessed:

The Unicorn Bookshop

One cultural gem that particularly embodied this community spirit was Bill Butler's Unicorn Bookshop, which stood at 50 Gloucester Road throughout the later decades of the nineteenth century. The store's exterior was nearly as infamous as the literary diversity it guarded inside. John Upton's large mural depicting moon, stars, rainbows and the rising sun spilled across the face of the building, and from the second floor of the shop a projected cavorting unicorn inspired life into the grey pavement below. Unicorn Bookshop:

[...] catered for all things underground: posters, hippy beads, bells, US beat poetry magazines and contemporary fiction. This was one of the first and very few places where a reader could peruse from America the *Evergreen Review*,

Unicorn bookshop c.1970s. Photo published in *Frendz* Magazine, 26 May 1972 by Mike Halliday.

Kulcher, the *Los Angeles Free Press*, Olympia press publications, the writings of William Burroughs, Jack Kerouac, Allen Ginsberg and Lawrence Ferlinghetti. [17]

Barry Pitman recalls the customers as "a mix of the 'local hippy' contingent in Brighton at that time, people interested in the counterculture and changing the world."[18] Regular visitors also included those looking for "alternative lifestyle info" and Sussex University students and academics searching for "alternative literature and sci-fi."[19] Patrick Newley recollects his first visit to the bookshop in the late 1960s:

Bill, a cultural icon himself, swiftly moved into publishing a "considerable number of books and pamphlets on subjects as varied as macrobiotic cookery, alternative Brighton, survival techniques, magic, esoterica and comics",[21] using the shop as his literary base. The shop owner also wrote poetry and science fiction for many years. The Unicorn Bookshop even sought to support other alternative ventures in the city, publishing radical co-operative Infinity Foods' first book *Nature's Foods* written by founder Pete Deadman.

In its later years, the Unicorn was involved in a number of controversies with local police for "obscene" stock and Butler was drawn into an expensive legal suit. Yet empathetic friends, fellow writers, academics and shop regulars continued to support and rally alongside Bill, with a circulated letter of appeal later turning into the 1970 collection *For Bill Butler* edited by Eric Mottram and Larry Wallrich.

Unicorn persevered. Underground newspapers were "supplied by a new underground press distributor called Frit Freight, run by Paul Garner [et al.]" and were circulated locally.[22] Events such as picnics and poetry recitals were suggested by the community and facilitated by the shop. Barry Pitman remembers: "Discussion groups often sprang up, anarchist groups

[...] the Little Red Schoolbook was also distributed from Unicorn. Local 'community-based' publications such as *Attila* were made there."[23] The shop's famous counter-culture visitors illustrated its continual relevance within alternative circles:

Behind the scenes financial issues plagued the business, eventually forcing Bill and his Unicorn co-owners to call it a day. The group left Brighton and moved to a remote cottage 'Nant Gwilw' in Wales, running a little commune and publishing books from their rural barn. Bill died on the 21st October 1977 in his Shepherd's Bush flat, but the cause of death remained "unascertained". The shop in Gloucester Road "spluttered on until 1975"[25] under new ownership, but eventually disappeared under the council remodelling at the western end of the street.

Public House Bookshop

Thankfully Unicorn's demise was softened by the blossoming of Richard Cupidi's Public House Bookshop, that was "more than willing to pick up the alternative baton [...] a legacy that was equal parts

Richard Cupidi, Lee-Harwood, Allen Ginsberg and Peter Orlovsky outside the Public House Bookshop, late 70s or early 80s by Richard Cupidi.

shamanic talking stick, joint and protest banner."[26] The initial location of 21 Little Preston Street didn't seem particularly promising at first glance: "it was [previously] an old traditional pub, The Dependant, which had been converted into a corkscrew factory for a few years and then left derelict for several more.

[...] The roof was damaged. The first floor was a sooty puddle."[27] But with a few licks of paint and Neal Dean's iconic alchemical mural, the shop became another alternative literary epicentre for Brighton and Hove. Owner Cupidi proudly reflects on the building's striking exterior:

> ‘Once you found Little Preston Street though, you couldn't miss the bookshop – a gleaming yellow Victorian public house, encased in salvaged Caterpillar Yellow enamel tractor paint. On the front wall where the brewer's brand had been, artist Neil Dean painted a Durer-inspired book with a porthole inside for viewing the universe. Directly above the mural was written one of our favourite Public House principles: *The book should be a ball of light in your hands.*’ [28]

This bold façade ensured that the shop stood apart from the mounting competition of Brighton and Hove's other booksellers. By the mid 1970s, Public House was met with rivalry from Bredon's and Beal's, Robinson's Quadrant, Brighton Books, Combridge's and Practical Books amongst others. The emphasis Cupidi placed on nurturing an alternative community ensured that, like Unicorn, Public House was never short of loyal customers. The shop owner explicitly prioritised the emotional and intellectual development of the collective:

> ‘Good independent bookshops like [Public House] are congregational spaces, rich in potential encounters and communities. They embody the voices of individual books amplified into coalitions of dialogue;

they generate communities of readers, of searchers, Greek choruses of the curious. For many people, going to Public House was an emotional experience as well as a cognitive one – they saw it as an oasis of expectations. For others, [Public House] was a sanctuary space or the embodiment of resistance.' [29]

Such radical openness and acceptance of alternative beliefs was not met with universal approval and Public House was confronted by a handful of local cynics over the years. Traditionalists, particularly in the form of The National Front and local splinter groups, were widely considered responsible for the attempted fire-bombing of the building:

'Within a year of opening, Public House had been fire-bombed. [...] Luckily it landed in such a way that the firework fuse burnt against the sturdy wooden door and eventually went out, failing to properly ignite.' [30]

Public House continued on regardless. Indeed, in a letter written by Cupidi and other bookshop staff, the owner accentuated his pride in the shop's ability to challenge the local community by sparking offence, or simply a reconsideration of personal prejudice:

'For more than twenty-five years the Public House Bookshop has informed, stimulated, irritated, encouraged, inspired, intellectually fed and emotionally watered many people. It moved poets

Drawing of the Public House Bookshop by Richard Cupidi.

The shop ensured the preservation and perpetuation of many of the "pockets of alternative culture surviving from the 1960s",[32] working alongside local events, societies and festivals. Cupidi argued: "The Basement […] served as a performance space, quiet room, rehearsal room, a space for art installations, a cinema and a crèche."[33] It comes as no surprise that Public House Bookshop attracted a range of local 70s and 80s radicals. The shop was frequently loud and actively engaged with the community, working alongside Brighton's Resource Centre and other venues to "create opportunities galore. A Women's Book week and related events were proposed, advertised and successfully held in 1984 […]."[34] Yet Public House never failed to neglect its primary source of trading, with the "books and magazines in the shop remain[ing] the finest selection outside London."[35] Cupidi's passion for Native American cultures, artwork and storytelling brought another radically different aspect to the shop floor.

It was even rumoured that Anita Roddick, the businesswoman who started up natural cosmetics chain The Body Shop, sourced many of her natural remedy recipes from books found at the back of Public House. The shop was the first in Brighton to stock and circulate alternative quarterly journals such as *Talking Stick*, *Gay News*, *Quim* and *Spare Rib*.

However, the business continued to juggle specialities beyond books and magazines: "It became a polyphonic circus of voices: independent music, especially free jazz, on vinyl and in performance; small press poetry on the page, recorded and in performance; art, photography and graphics installations, with live events by the artists; storytelling and spoken word events."[36]

Unfortunately, the rise of commercial booksellers made the running of Public House Bookshop a continual uphill battle. After being cherished as a linchpin of the Brighton community for just shy of three decades, last orders were called in 1999. Cupidi's final letter perfectly summarised both Public House's radical presence in Brighton and the vital importance of alternative spaces in local communities: "To those of you who have never known this place, let's hope that there will always be environments like this one – fired with passion, creativity, a pleasure in people and in the power of words."[37]

Symposium and Solstice

One of Public House's notable bookshop comrades was Symposium. Located at 12 Market Square in the Lanes area, Symposium, similar to the other alternative bookshops of the period, converted the upstairs space into an art gallery and exhibition space, encouraging local artists to display their work.

This renovated space provided the location for one of Sean Sprague's early photography showcases. In 1974 the shop published a slim poetry anthology *Open Door* that included translations of French poets Rimbaud and Apollinaire. Shire explains that Symposium:

> **'** […] continued [Bill] Butler's successful, if legally risky, strategy of importing from the US. While Butler knew East Coast beat poets personally, Symposium dealt with important West Coast distributors, bringing in science fiction, poetry, and studies in spirituality, magic and radical politics […].**'** [38]

Financial issues forced the owners to relocate to 28 Trafalgar Street in the spring of 1977 under a new name, 'Solstice'. Symposium's identity changes were reflected in the wider community, as Brighton itself was undergoing a process of metamorphosis, with cultural shifts underway: "The punks took over from the hippies as the hippies had taken over from the beats, the mods and rockers."[39]

In its new North Laine home, Solstice continued to draw in an alternative crowd with a radical range of reading material including "poetry, mysticism, psychotherapy and the occult […] martial arts selections, underground commix […] guitar and other specialist magazines […]."[40] Solstice also worked closely alongside other bookshops to ensure the materialisation of many local arts events. In 1979, Public House teamed up with Solstice to successfully organise a poetry reading by Allen Ginsberg and Peter Orlovsky at the Lanes' Meeting House.

Despite its significant local popularity, "grinding economics"[41] crushed Solstice's legacy. Owner Paul had a family and children to support, and as Shire bluntly asserts: "alternative bookselling has never been a way to get rich."[42]

Other Bookshops of Note

Other alternative booksellers were drastically unconventional in their distribution of Gay Literature. *Daring Hearts'* contributor James recalls one particular bookseller:

Michael's inconspicuous style of dealing with risqué subject matter was not taken as standard practice for all local booksellers. James goes on to remember: "[…] in North Road, there was what they used to call a dirty bookshop, which you'll never find now, where everything was cellophane wrapped and they would have all these ghastly books in the window. 'Miss Whiplash' and all that sort of thing."[44] Regardless of their antithetical trading styles, the very existence of these booksellers emulated Brighton's radically unprejudiced attitude to sexual orientation as early as the 1970s, providing spaces for sexual exploration and discovery.

Though the unapologetic cultural attitudes of the 1970s and 80s proved to be the perfect hotbed for Brighton's alternative book trade, a few glimmers of that era are still retained by a handful of local shops. Alongside distributing a wonderful array of literature, Kemptown Bookshop at 91 St. George's Road is affiliated with The Bookroom Arts Press. The press is a small publishers and printers that specialise in reproduction prints of artists from The Grosvenor School, Neo-Romantic School and Pop Art movements. Kemptown Bookshop explains:

(left) Logo of
Kemptown Bookshop,
2019 by Evlynn Sharp.

(below) City Books,
2019 by Evlynn Sharp.

' The name 'The Bookroom Art Press' derives from 'The Bookroom' where it was first housed – a room which comprised one story of the Bookshop. Our premises are now at Portland Place, Kemptown, but the Bookshop still acts as main world-wide distributor for the Press [...]. '[45]

Though not quite as radical as Butler and Cupidi's homemade printing presses, the close co-existence between store and printing press echoes the alternative diversity of earlier bookshops.

City Books on Western Road encapsulates the treasure-trove style of bookshop that Unicorn and Public House exemplified. Run by Paul and Inge Sweetman, the independent shop saddles the best of the old and new bookshops in order to financially keep its head above water. The owners outline their ethos: "We pride ourselves in our traditional values, whilst using the best of modern technology to provide excellent service, delivered with a light touch."[46] City Books frequently runs literary events that allow audiences to listen to readings of up-and-coming books and enter into conversation with writers.

Though both these modern bookshops are far removed from the liberating Bacchanal and tantalisingly alternative evenings of intimate 80s Ginsberg recitals, their attempts to directly engage with the arts narrative of the Brighton community is to be applauded, considering the restraints placed on them by the oppressive shadow of online retail.

Notes

1 https://queensparkbooks.org. uk/about-2.

2 QueenSpark Women Writers, *Writers Reign* (Brighton: QueenSpark Books, 1991).

3 Ibid.

4 QueenSpark Stroke Writing Group, *Life after Stroke* (Brighton: QueenSpark Books, 1993).

5 *Life after Stroke*.

6 Tillie Olsen, *Silences*.

7 Dawn Bartram, Margaret Bearfield, Marion Devoy et al., *Stories from the Nights at the Round Table* (Brighton: QueenSpark Books, 1998).

8 *QueenSpark Women Writers* (Brighton: QueenSpark Books, 1984).

9 Ibid.

10 Ibid.

11 Ibid.

12 Ibid.

13 Ibid.

14 John Shire, *Bookends: A Partial History of the Brighton Book Trade* (Brighton: Invocations Press, 2011), p. 7.

15 Ibid. pp. 15-16.

16 Ibid. p. 60.

17 Ibid. p. 39.

18 Barry Pitman, contributor.

19 Ibid.

20 Peter Dennis, Beccie Mannall and Linda Pointing, *Daring Hearts* (Brighton: QueenSpark Books in collaboration with Brighton Ourstory, 1992).

21 Barry Pitman.

22 *Bookends*, p. 49.

23 Barry Pitman.

24 *Bookends*, p. 48.

25 Ibid. p. 56.

26 Ibid. p. 61.

27 Ibid. p. 73.

28 Richard Cupidi, 'The Intrepid Bookseller of Brighton'.

29 Ibid.

30 *Bookends*, p. 75.

31 'Intrepid Bookseller'.

32 Jonathan M. Woodham, Neil Butler, Roger Ely et al., *ZAP: Twenty-Five years of Innovation* (Brighton: QueenSpark Books, 2007).

33 'Intrepid Bookseller'.

34 *Bookends*, p. 79.

35 Ibid. p. 80.

36 'Intrepid Bookseller'.

37 Ibid.

38 *Bookends*, p. 62.

39 Ibid. p. 63.

40 Ibid. p. 66.

41 Ibid. p. 69.

42 Ibid. p. 69.

43 *Daring Hearts*.

44 Ibid.

45 http://www. kemptownbookshop.co.uk.

46 http://www.city-books.co.uk.

Kemptown Bookshop shopfront, 2019 by Evlynn Sharp.

extinction
rebellion
POLITICAL
SPACES

chapter 2

Lisa Redlinski & Davy Jones

Lisa Redlinski & Davy Jones

THIS HISTORY IS WRITTEN TO APPLAUD THE radical culture of Brighton and the ordinary Lefties who challenged and won the contest of values in the city's public debates. The primary sources of progressive British political discourse are scattered and difficult to identify. This map to the historic avenues of Lefty culture in Brighton puts the Left in a broad perspective.

The terms "Lefty" and "progressive" are interchangeable, based on the definition of moral politics as written by Dr. George Lakoff, the University of Berkeley's Distinguished Professor of Cognitive Linguistics. To summarise Lakoff, Lefty values are understood as those which support public resources, the environment, civic rights, freedom, fairness, personal happiness, and nurturing justice. This worldview is in contrast to the conservative moral hierarchy which is the rich above the poor, Western culture above other cultures, men above women, whites above non-whites, straights above gays, and employers above employees.[1]

How Brighton became characterised as a city of hippie immanence and Lefty numen has answers in an eighteenth-century doctor, a 1930s chimney sweep, and in the corpus of 1960s-90s grassroots papers.

To see how extraordinary it is to have this sparkling jewel of a progressive town, put it in the perspective of other coastal communities. From the fifteenth century, English fishing communities endured relentless poverty due to coastal erosion, raiding ships, and a decline in the demand for fish. The world did not visit Brighton to create culture, it came to extract feudal payments and for conquest. In the sixteenth century the

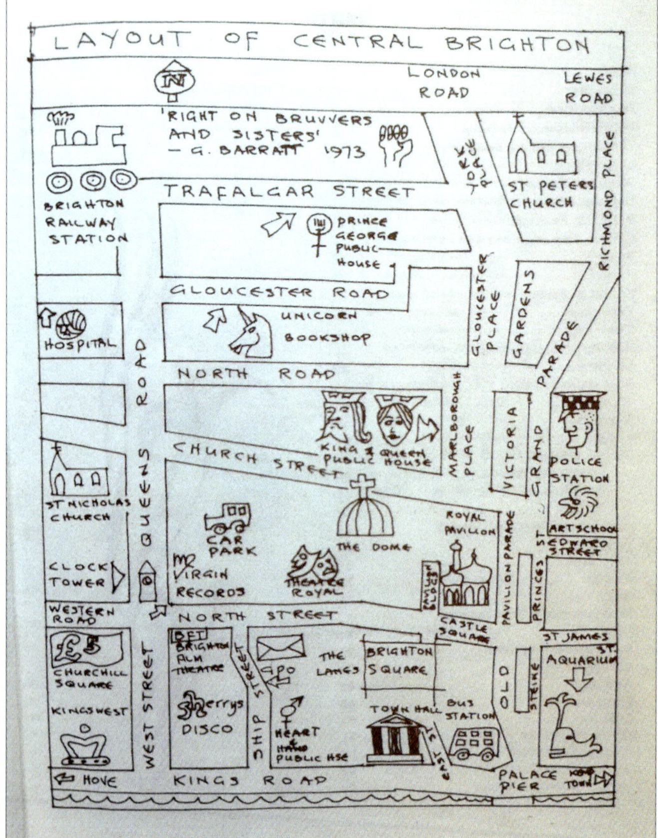

Layout of central Brighton.

parish of Brighton had collapsed and privations lasted centuries. Brighton needed a miracle if it was ever going to become one for anybody. The miracle happened in the eighteenth century, thanks to the age-old remedy of Nature's Cure.

Doctor Richard Russell attended to the well-heeled of Lewes. Suffering from conditions which seemed untreatable, he prescribed a curative day at Brighton's beach. The patients took their scripts and their shillings to eat, to sleep, and to shop in Brighton. By 1777 Brighton was a fashionable health resort – albeit one with unpopular officials such as its Master of Ceremonies who "promulgated rules within the town, even, in 1787, prohibiting the playing of games on the Steine on penalty of a fine."[2]

After Brighton developed its hospitality industry, local trades such as transport, lighting, and building employed people. While the labourers were still in poverty, the *noblesse oblige* of the wealthy tourists supported public institutions, such as Countess de Noailles[3] funding in 1856 of a library and lecture room with room for 600 occupants on 43 Essex Street. In 1885 "Milky Edwards" was elected as a workers' councillor and by 1890 a local Trades Council formed out of 14 branches. The first organised grassroots response to dispossession happened around 1920 thanks to a "best-known and best-loved" of the Brighton men, Harry Cowley. "A chimney-sweep by trade but a champion of the traders, the poor, the elderly and the homeless,"[4] Mr. Cowley was the public voice for a historic squatting movement where people seized empty properties for the homeless. Brighton Lefties invented the squatting technique.

Today there is an anarchist community centre named in Mr. Cowley's honour.

By the 1950s, a mature middle class with a social conscience grew its first network of connected roots in Brighton. People were insured by the NHS, politicised by unions, branded by Holtham's peace symbol, informed by Campaign for Nuclear Disarmament reports about the threats of nuclear power, and protesting against Aldermaston. A growing segment of Brighton's population took responsibility to institutionalise these hard-earned rights.

By the 1960s, a sizeable, educated, cultured, middle-class youth had a little bit of spending money, and lot of new technologies. Amplifiers, light machines, recording and broadcast equipment, all electrified a party scene. For the first time in history home printing was possible. As analogue as a spindle, the mimeograph allowed anyone to be published.

The University of Sussex enrolled its first intake in 1961 and taught left-wing egalitarian political theory. People came to study in Brighton from India, China, and the United States. The city was no longer boxed in; the world was visiting Brighton.

But there was still a strong element in the city of right-wing politics. For example, Julian Amery, Tory MP for Brighton Pavilion from 1969-1992, was a member of the far right Monday Club. On one memorable afternoon in a Saltdean Conservative election meeting, a young voter, Davy Jones, was in attendance and queried whether it was true that Mr. Amery's

Bertrand Russell leads an anti-nuclear march, London, 1961 by Tony French.

ATTILA is a community newspaper. That means you provide whatever goes into it. Stories, letters, whatever, to UNICORN where they'll be put into the next issue. Try to keep items short so we can get a lot in.

Attila Issue 3, 1971.

brother, John Amery, was executed after the war for being a Nazi. Mr. Jones was punched in the face by the gentleman seated in front of him.[5] It was widely believed that fascists ran at least two hotels on the seafront and were active in attacking alternative establishments and bookshops. The first Infinity Foods warehouse burnt down mysteriously too in the 1970s, though the investigation was inconclusive.

For those who liked their political friendships to be based on apartheid, the earthy alternative groups were a chance to bring their massacre and brutality dreams to life. Grown men kicked at the nearest wobble of a beanpole vegetarian.

In 1966 an American named Bill Butler opened Unicorn Bookshop, a radical bookshop at 50 Gloucester Road. Raunchy and subversive, Mr. Butler welcomed visitors asking, "Can I help you locate some *filthy* books." People visited for extemporaneous political dialogue. Many people walked out with sets of local press papers. Mr. Butler and his staff edited, authored, and cranked out their paper *Attila* among other titles such as *Leaves of Grass*, a self-authored marijuana cookbook. He ran a small printing service on behalf of commissioning customers who were keen to make their own posters, fliers, and newspapers.

Even though the shop was often annoyed by anonymous threats, Mr. Butler had a mission as "an honest statement in bookshop terms of what is actually going on." The blow that Mr. Butler never fully emotionally recovered from was a 1968 raid by police who seized materials they considered obscene such as Marquis du Sade and the famous *Schoolkids Oz* magazine. These copies were easily available in London bookshops, but in Brighton he was condemned for the crowd he drew in. Charged with a £2,700 fine, Mr. Butler returned to the bookshop and displayed the offensive materials in the shop window accompanied by Judge Ripper's commentary.[6] An ardent environmentalist, Mr. Butler decamped to Wales with his partner in the early 1970s. There is a mural commemorating Unicorn Bookshop on Gloucester Road today.

For a while, Richard Cupidi ran Unicorn Books with Mr. Butler. In 1972 Mr. Cupidi opened Public House Bookshop (PHB) in a building which he, alongside others, squatted and then leased. In Mr. Cupidi's impressionistic memoir he writes that radical bookshops were "congregational spaces, rich in potential encounters and communities."[7] His experience at Unicorn informed the design of the bookshop. PHB scheduled a series of lectures to which the general public was welcome. The casual violence of irate conservative reactionaries meant taking a formal assessment of the dangers. To take care of the staff, he installed a public-facing desk purpose-built as a defensive space, and the employee training programme included self-defence classes.[8]

Effecting massive social change is difficult. The counter-culture was figuring out how to connect into the town's underground roots and give itself an overground home. An observer at the time writes: "Brighton is neither a quiet provincial backwater nor a solid Tory stronghold but a politically alive town."[9] 1970s Brighton underwent a surge of development, threatening to build a new commercialism over the fledgling grassroots spaces. City planning underwrote the already established class divisions between neighbourhoods, and the council withheld investment in poor areas and enhanced the wealthy ones.

In a popular grassroots publication, *Alternative Brighton* 1973, the introductory chapter starts with a call to participate in town planning:

> 'Vast changes to the physical structure of our towns are increasingly taking place. These changes have a far-reaching effect on society and yet are brought about by, and in the interests of, a small powerful and affluent minority. We indicate here the issues and consequences in Brighton, and the possible ways in which individuals and the community might organise to stop, change or redefine plans which will affect them.' [10]

The Brighton Urban Structures city plan started a fight for better city development strategies. And it set the stage for intergroup campaigning. The working-class and counter-culture amplified one another's voices for a shared vision for Brighton. Selma Montfort, art teacher at Brighton Polytechnic and later the founder and director of its Urban Studies Department, and mother of four, took the mic.

Mrs. Montfort wrote *Disappearing Beauties of*

The Public House Bookshop, 1970s by Richard Cupidi.

ATTILA, 26 June I97I

MORE ALTERNATIVE ORGANIZING...
" Public House ", on the seafront end of Little Preston Street,
yellow building, opening in three weeks time.   Basically a centre
for information exchange, including a bookshop (cheap) which should
eventually wind up with its own free reference library, a coffee
space & a print/printing workshop to simplify the process and control
our own feedback.   Also organising a Peoples Yellow Pages - a
directory of individuals and groups who can, or know how to, provide
alternative services and skills : can we create our own jobs?   If
you want to be listed - everybody can do <u>something</u>, send them the
info with a few relevant details.   You are also needed to help put
the Yellow Pages together in a few weeks.   Now you know.   WHY is
it that most constructive vibes appear to come from AMERICAN heads?
They seem to have a better idea of the urgency of our situation...
Book now for the Doom & Disaster Trip, etc etc., but it ain't a
joke.   By the way, Public House will be open at weekends and also
a few nites during the week, so tomorrow can't have been cancelled,
no matter what the guy sez His name is.

Opening of Public House Bookshop announced in *Attila*, 1971.

Brighton[11], a walking tour of cat creeps, twittens, and secret parks. The tour uncovered the veiled treasures of the city and connected locals to centuries of emotion, the feelings of those before them who saw how freedom and pride could build a neighbourhood. Her articles were published in the alternative papers and her reliable presence at the council's planning meetings established her as a much-needed new guard for Brighton's environment. Her efforts were instrumental in saving Brighton Station and its gorgeous Mocatta Arches from redevelopment into flats and a car park. Then she was a heavyweight in the fight that saved Queen's Park.

At one point, developers proposed a casino in the Hanover area of Brighton. Queen's Park was the heart of the working-class neighbourhood. Walking distance from two primary schools and a pre-school, the residents preferred a nursery to a casino. The developers insisted on the casino. After a surge of community action, reported through radical press, the city ensured that a crèche was put in the park and the casino was instead located by the pier and so grouped with the other adult night-life attractions. The blueprints for Brighton Urban Structures city planning were deposited in the city council, but the blueprints drafted by the local community were deposited in its 70s local press.

Local papers did not set out strategic messaging campaigns outlining the values, principles, and progressive framing for its politics. Yet they were imbued by them; care for the environment, people over profits, equality, nurturing families, and personal happiness were values that dominated the discourse of popular culture. The invitation to contribute to the local story was sent to everyone. The counter-culture practised the principles that reflect those values – participatory democracy, investing in the common good, contributing our fair share, broad-based prosperity, ethical business and values-based policies.

People depended on alternative papers for news of protests, performances, and parties. These calendars of events in papers imprinted the city with its trademark environmentalism; alternative health practices; the macrobiotic foods movement; cycling as anti-car protest; international film cinema screenings; support networks for the vulnerable; gay rights; a festival scene. People often printed their or their parents' address and phone numbers and drew one another closer, breaking free from consumer culture's radioactive belts of isolation.

The index for *Alternative Brighton* is an A-Z of the hallmarks of local identities that makes Brighton the progressive city it is today. The guide was edited by John Noyce and Francis Jarman with a battalion of contributors. From the index we can see how many political and inspired concepts had landed in Brighton – everything from Buddhists, Family Planning, Gay & Transsexual, Hitching, Nature Cure & Sport, to the Working Association for Mothers.

Learning about points of interest for the counter-culture is just one of many lessons from these papers. The radical press shows us how to frame Lefty policies. It shows us that propaganda is a necessary and good thing when its message is more true than prevailing mainstream beliefs.

Community campaign in *QueenSpark* newsletter, 1972.

A school year's worth of lessons can be learned from these papers. They gave young people a chance to be critical and expressive, while also being ok with one another's occasional wrongness. The closure of papers occurred for many reasons. One area of historical examination that will help inform the Left today, is how often papers folded because people became more strident in their beliefs at the expense of giving room to other people's less articulated, freewheeling, impressionistic expressions.

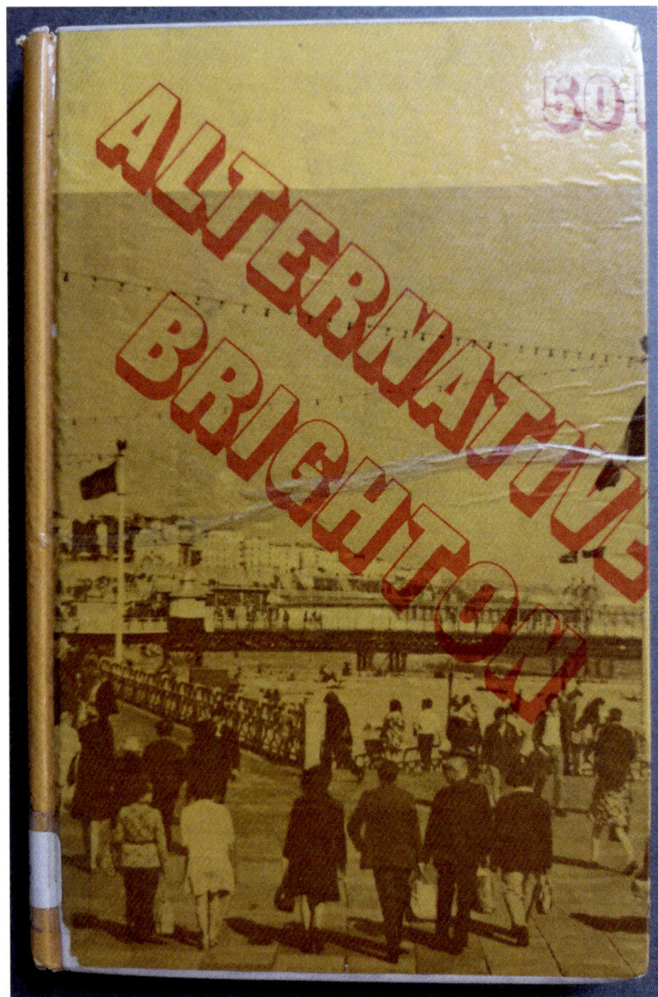

Alternative Brighton guide.

The highly participatory culture allowed young people to practise their enterprising skillset. Creating a public space for people to publish their texts, and the responses from the public, was a breakthrough. The progressive NOW of Brighton is growing from these roots – Caroline Lucas, the UK's only Green parliamentary member, the anarchist centre Cowley Club, community-run pubs and centres such as The Bevy, Exeter Street Hall, and Rose Hill Tavern. Infinity Foods, Queen's Park, Brighton Station concourse and many more places, people, and events which come and go are tracks that connect back to this movement.

These papers were not collected systematically by libraries, and so there is no single archive to dig through for UK papers (though there is for the US radical press[12]). There are, however, several sources for these papers. Harvester Press – a Brighton-based publisher – micro-photographed 131 UK titles in the Underground Press Collection, which is available at the University of Brighton. John Spiers, the head of Harvester Press, deposited his archive at The Keep. The Cowley Club also has a library with many of these titles available as reading, some of which are being digitised by their committed volunteer staff.

Many regional titles are hiding away in attics and closets of collectors and no longer available to the public. One such collector is John May[13], who has a comprehensive private archive that includes the first ephemera for Glastonbury, a taped interview with Polish writer Richard Kapuściński, and a copy of *The Index of Possibilities* (the UK version of the *Whole Earth Catalogue*).

Where possible, regional titles are digitised and put on the Radical Brighton blog.[14] *Attila, Fly, Librarians for Social Change* are online. Many titles cited in alternative papers that are digitised are absent from online repositories. There are major characters from the radical Brighton scene who are invisible in the archives and remembered only through oral history. Jenny Harris and her radical theatre group Brighton Combination is certainly one such example. Her personality and contribution to the scene are far greater than those little fly-postings would have us believe. To bring together these papers with oral history, in the frame of a broad conceptual Left framework, allows us to give context to material and people that are otherwise invisible.

The context for these papers is political, just as the papers are. In Brighton there was a culture of strict austerity paternalism until a mass of people created a new culture. Alternative papers document these active forms of public discourse.

A chronological sampling of Brighton's alternative papers

As the bibliographic information on some of these papers is somewhat lacking and gleaned from bits of information found in the papers themselves, this is a suggestion of possible start and end dates.

Head and Freak 1968
In 1968, John Upton, Brighton's beloved counter-cultural muralist and illustrator, published a mimeo mag (foolscap-size pages printed roneo/gestetner one side).

What's On Where; Matchbox 1969?
Entertainment/events papers citation found in *Alternative Brighton* 1973.

Dis; Brush; 1985 1969?
University student press citation to titles found in *Alternative Brighton* 1973.

Fly 1969
Brighton, Hove & Sussex Grammar School student Davy Jones invited his friends to contribute to a school paper, mimeographed at Unicorn Bookshop. Copies on the Radical Brighton blog.[15] Mr. Jones published in other titles such as *Attila* and embodies what he writes about – that we should all do our share.

Harvester/Primary Social Sources

The Underground and Alternative Press in Britain

A Bibliographical Guide with historical notes

By John Spiers

Published with a title and chronological index as a companion to the Underground/ Alternative Press collection prepared for microform publication by Ann Sexsmith and Alastair Everitt

THE HARVESTER PRESS 1974

John May, 1972.

(above) Covers of *Fly*, 1969.

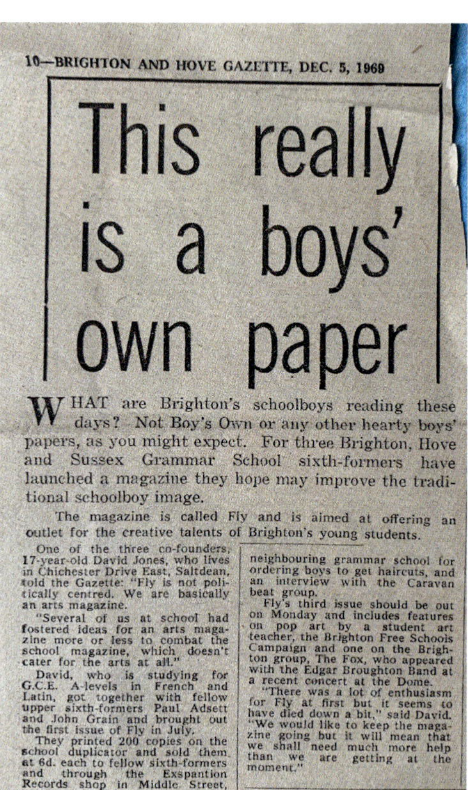

10—BRIGHTON AND HOVE GAZETTE, DEC. 5, 1969

This really is a boys' own paper

WHAT are Brighton's schoolboys reading these days? Not Boy's Own or any other hearty boys' papers, as you might expect. For three Brighton, Hove and Sussex Grammar School sixth-formers have launched a magazine they hope may improve the traditional schoolboy image.

The magazine is called Fly and is aimed at offering an outlet for the creative talents of Brighton's young students.

One of the three co-founders, 17-year-old David Jones, who lives in Chichester Drive East, Saltdean, told the Gazette: "Fly is not politically centred. We are basically an arts magazine.

"Several of us at school had fostered ideas for an arts magazine more or less to combat the school magazine, which doesn't cater for the arts at all."

David, who is studying for G.C.E. A-levels in French and Latin, got together with fellow upper sixth-formers Paul Adsett and John Grain and brought out the first issue of Fly in July.

They printed 200 copies on the school duplicator and sold them at 6d. each to fellow sixth-formers and through the Exspantion Records shop in Middle Street, Brighton.

Among the articles in the first two issues was an attack on a neighbouring grammar school for ordering boys to get haircuts, and an interview with the Caravan beat group.

Fly's third issue should be out on Monday and includes features on pop art by a student art teacher, the Brighton Free Schools Campaign and one on the Brighton group, The Fox, who appeared with the Edgar Broughton Band at a recent concert at the Dome.

"There was a lot of enthusiasm for Fly at first but it seems to have died down a bit," said David. "We would like to keep the magazine going but it will mean that we shall need much more help than we are getting at the moment."

(right) News cutting about *Fly*, *Brighton & Hove Gazette*, 1969.

Friends 1969

Friends came out of London and was London's main source of alternative news reporting. Lewes resident John May was one of its main editors and contributors. *Friends* was part of the triptych of major alternative papers *It* and *Oz*, covering music such as Hawkwind and the Pink Fairies; festivals such as Bath, Isle of Wight, Phun City, Glastonbury, and Bickershaw; drug culture; the esoteric; the White Panthers; Malcolm X; and trials embroiling radicals.

This paper is in itself a case study for how papers on the Left would, in turn, illuminate and destroy. Capable of profound insights into complex discourses of power, it then punched holes in its own intellectual hull by publishing pornography which allowed men to embarrass women and the values that nurturing relationships stood for.

Attila 1971

A community effort, dozens of self-described "nuisance freaks" contributed to the paper. Brighton historian and local everyman luminary in his own right, Paul Kaczmarek, wrote about *Attila*:

> ❛Rik is Rik Wilkins, a big burly biker with a fierce Viking beard and a gentle laughing stoner temperament. He did almost all the mock-up and printing work for *Attila* and most of the other duplicated publications between late 1970 and early 1972 on the ancient smelly machinery upstairs at the shop. ❜ [16]

Bill Butler moved to Brighton from London. He was in San Francisco during at least 1955-9, and haunted the infamous City Lights Bookshop there, where he met Ginsberg, Kerouac and the rest of the Beat Poets. Bill kept a lifelong contact with a number of them – Ginsberg performed a reading at Unicorn. From there Bill went to Greece in late '59, where he taught English and worked on a traffic scheme for the authorities, went back to SF and published his first book early 1960, then moved to London sometime late 1960 – the records are very sketchy on dates before 1962.

While in London, he was involved with the alternative literature scene, and in 1965 managed the paperback section of Better Books, the classic early 60s alternative literary bookshop in the UK. He left them in early November 1965 and moved to Brighton, where he was a bookrunner for about a year before setting up Unicorn Bookshop, which opened Summer 1967. Letters addressed to Bill at his permanent address 12 Over Street, Brighton (just across from Unicorn) exist from 12th November 1965; the first Unicorn letters or invoices date from early August 1967.

Librarians for Social Change 1973

In 1973 three just-hatched radicals lived in a flat on Vere Road, Brighton, one of whom was John Noyce, founder of Librarians for Social Change (LfSC).[17] In LfSC John collected together articles and comics penned by librarians across Britain. John printed the LfSC issues with the hand powered mimeograph that he stashed under his bed. Copies were postal mailed out to anyone who paid their 20p.

LfSC writers were incensed by libraries which were unwilling to collect the out-of-the-ordinary print materials of radicals. Equally, LfSC writers were

Cover of *Attila*, 1971. From Davy Jones.

. . . . .

A MACROBIOTIC FOOD SHOP at 54 Church Street. Just above Queen's Road. Grains, organic vegetables, seaweeds, Japanese foods, beans, teas, drinks, books, pots & pans, magazines, incense, chopsticks, chopping knives etc. Same people who do BITING THROUGH at the University are doing it.

A MACROBIOTIC RESTAURANT Planned for the bottom end of Trafalgar Street. If the Home Office can pull its Civil Service finger out.

OPEN SECT has opened. (And my secret love's no secret anymore). So far, thanks to lacking some piece of paper they're not allowed to stay open after 6. So try to fall by there before. They're also running a sort of RELEASE thing, about which I'll pass on more gen. when I have it.

RELEASE PHONE NUMBERS:
(01) 229-7753
(01) 727-7753

EMERGENCY(01) 603-8654

Another MAGICAL MYSTERY TOUR is being got together. Anybody wanting a nice ride somewhere with a bunch of congenial folk leave name & address at UNICORN=

Andy's throwing another party for kids across the street from the cop shop Saturday afternoon.....2:30? Should be one of the nicer parts of the Festival. (FESTIVAL? of WHAT?)

FREE CONCERT at Churchill Square, Saturday Afternoon, 2 p.m. Red Head Yorke & assorted freakes. Make it.

HOT MANNA forming in Lewes. ARTS LAB cum RELEASE set-up. Very little money, very little equipment, but trying. If you've got ideas or anything they might need write Nasso, HOT MANNA, 57 SOUTH STREET, LEWES= No phone as yet as they're in shared digs.

Donations of most clothing items in aid of victims of the recent disasters should continue to be made to OXFAM. Brassieres & other undergarments may, however, be sent directly to BRIGHTON POLICE STATION, JOHN STREET, BRIGHTON. Every attempt will be made to see that they are directed to the right people.

Page from the first issue of *Attila*, 1971.

First edition of *Librarians for Social Change.*

First edition cover of *A Woman's Place?,* 1973.

energised by the potential of libraries as progressive centres in otherwise conservative communities.

At that time, there was still a considerable group of fascist residents in Brighton. Radicals wanted to openly challenge that value system.

John was an avid collector of radical press. His metal shelves overflowed with stacks of local press papers. John's apprehensive landlord grew uneasy with his tenancy. The titles' provocative language, characteristic of local press at that time, made him doubt John's integrity. He asked John to vacate the flat.

Most library managers, like John's landlord, were reluctant to adapt progressive policies. Whether or not LfSC was successful in their work to pave inroads for radical print culture into British libraries remains to be decided. It is certain, though, that LfSC built friendships among librarians. You can feel the shared frustration of these sincere young librarians pouring off the LfSC pages.

John, along with his Vere Road roommate Francis Jarman, also wrote a comprehensive bibliography of radical playwright David Mercer[18] and the *Alternative Guide to Brighton*, 1973.

A Woman's Place? 1973
Brighton's first feminist radical paper.

Brighton Voice 1970s
Monthly paper published out of Clermont Terrace, considered one of the best local papers which arose out of the local Labour Party *Voice* but had a broader political base.

Datr 1970s
Edited by John Noyce (*Librarians for Social Change*; *Alternative Brighton* 1973), an irregular poetry

publication with international contributors. Citation from *Alternative Brighton* 1973.

Fleabite (5 issues as of 1973); Gutter Press (8 issues as of 1973)

Local anarchist papers, citations in *Alternative Brighton* 1973.

Bright Times 1976

Brighton magazine on the politics of liberation (copies in Underground Press Collection).

Rubicon 1981

From the issue in 1981: "Rubicon really is a paper of the people. Not just because people can buy it and read it but more importantly the *people can write and produce it.* We welcome contributions from writers artists poets and almost anyone with anything they feel they want to communicate to the people of Brighton via this medium… We hope it will play some part in driving away the wet fog of apathy that dissipates the spark of life in the motor of our consciousness."

ECA Preston Circus Association 1981

First issue 1981.

Outreach (Student Union) 1983

Sussex Students' Union paper, first issue 1983?

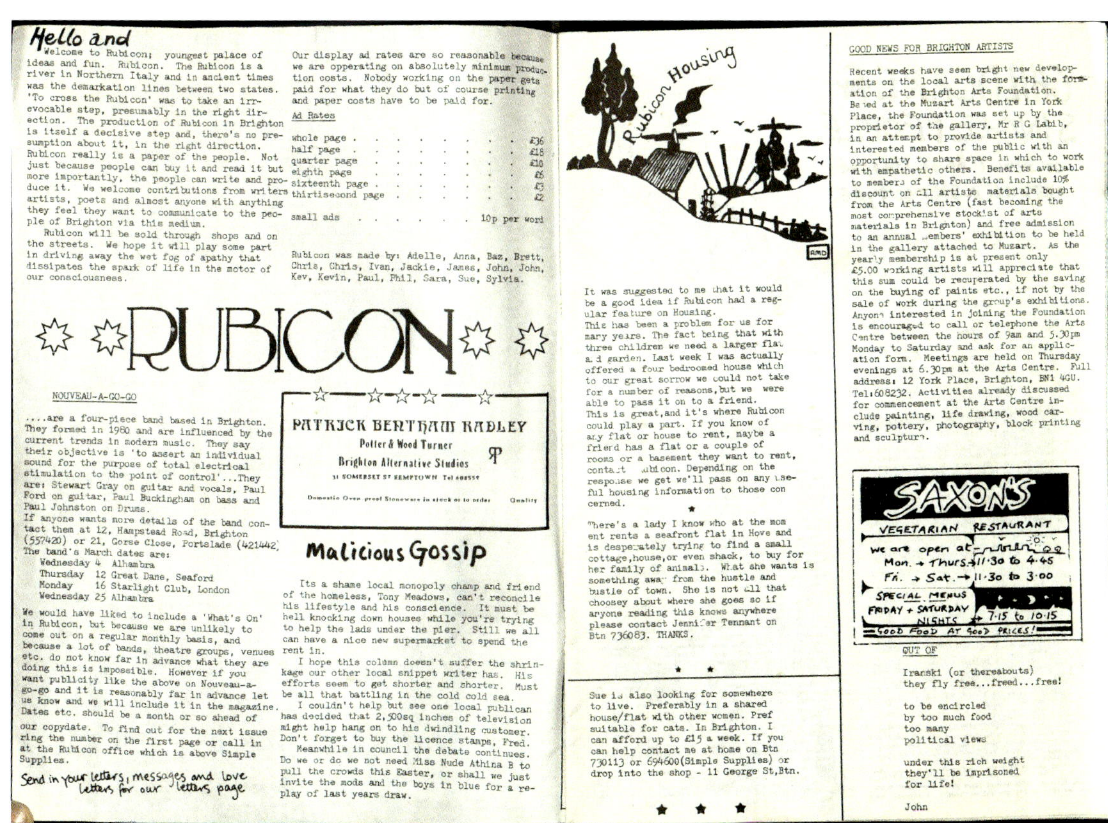

Hello and

Welcome to Rubicon; youngest palace of ideas and fun. Rubicon. The Rubicon is a river in Northern Italy and in ancient times was the demarkation lines between two states. 'To cross the Rubicon' was to take an irrevocable step, presumably in the right direction. The production of Rubicon in Brighton is itself a decisive step and, there's no presumption about it, in the right direction. Rubicon really is a paper of the people. Not just because people can buy it and read it but more importantly, the people can write and produce it. We welcome contributions from writers artists, poets and almost anyone with anything they feel they want to communicate to the people of Brighton via this medium.

Rubicon will be sold through shops and on the streets. We hope it will play some part in driving away the wet fog of apathy that dissipates the spark of life in the motor of our consciousness.

Our display ad rates are so reasonable because we are opperating on absolutely minimum production costs. Nobody working on the paper gets paid for what they do but of course printing and paper costs have to be paid for.

Ad Rates

whole page	£36
half page	£18
quarter page	£10
eighth page	£6
sixteenth page	£3
thirtisecond page	£2
small ads	10p per word

Rubicon was made by: Adelle, Anna, Baz, Brett, Chris, Chris, Ivan, Jackie, James, John, John, Kev, Kevin, Paul, Phil, Sara, Sue, Sylvia.

RUBICON

NOUVEAU-A-GO-GO

….are a four-piece band based in Brighton. They formed in 1980 and are influenced by the current trends in modern music. They say their objective is 'to assert an individual sound for the purpose of total electrical stimulation to the point of control'…They are: Stewart Gray on guitar and vocals, Paul Ford on guitar, Paul Buckingham on bass and Paul Johnston on Drums.

If anyone wants more details of the band contact them at 12, Hampstead Road, Brighton (557420) or 21, Gorse Close, Portslade (421442). The band's March dates are:

Wednesday 4 Alhambra
Thursday 12 Great Dane, Seaford
Monday 16 Starlight Club, London
Wednesday 25 Alhambra

We would have liked to include a 'What's On' in Rubicon, but because we are unlikely to come out on a regular monthly basis, and because a lot of bands, theatre groups, venues etc. do not know far in advance what they are doing this is impossible. However if you want publicity like the above on Nouveau-a-go-go and it is reasonably far in advance let us know and we will include it in the magazine. Dates etc. should be a month or so ahead of our copydate. To find out for the next issue ring the number on the first page or call in at the Rubicon office which is above Simple Supplies.

Send in your letters, messages and love letters for our letters page

PATRICK BERTHAM RADLEY
Potter & Wood Turner
Brighton Alternative Studios
11 SOMERSET ST KEMPTOWN Tel 608559

Domestic Oven proof Stoneware in stock or to order   Quality

Malicious Gossip

Its a shame local monopoly champ and friend of the homeless, Tony Meadows, can't reconcile his lifestyle and his conscience. It must be hell knocking down houses while you're trying to help the lads under the pier. Still we all can have a nice new supermarket to spend the rent in.

I hope this column doesn't suffer the shrinkage our other local snippet writer has. His efforts seem to get shorter and shorter. Must be all that battling in the cold cold sea.

I couldn't help but see one local publican has decided that 2,500sq inches of television might help hang on to his dwindling customer. Don't forget to buy the licence stamps, Fred.

Meanwhile in council the debate continues. Do we or do we not need Miss Nude Athina B to pull the crowds this Easter, or shall we just invite the mods and the boys in blue for a replay of last years draw.

It was suggested to me that it would be a good idea if Rubicon had a regular feature on Housing.

This has been a problem for us for many years. The fact being that with three children we need a larger flat and garden. Last week I was actually offered a four bedroomed house which to our great sorrow we could not take for a number of reasons, but we were able to pass it on to a friend. This is great, and it's where Rubicon could play a part. If you know of any flat or house to rent, maybe a friend has a flat or a couple of rooms or a basement they want to rent, contact Rubicon. Depending on the response we get we'll pass on any useful housing information to those concerned.

There's a lady I know who at the moment rents a seafront flat in Hove and is desperately trying to find a small cottage, house, or even shack, to buy for her family of animals. What she wants is something away from the hustle and bustle of town. She is not all that choosey about where she goes so if anyone reading this knows anywhere please contact Jennifer Tennant on Btn 736083. THANKS.

Sue is also looking for somewhere to live. Preferably in a shared house/flat with other women. Pref suitable for cats. In Brighton. I can afford up to £15 a week. If you can help contact me at home on Btn 730113 or 694600(Simple Supplies) or drop into the shop - 11 George St, Btn.

GOOD NEWS FOR BRIGHTON ARTISTS

Recent weeks have seen bright new developments on the local arts scene with the formation of the Brighton Arts Foundation. Based at the Muzart Arts Centre in York Place, the Foundation was set up by the proprietor of the gallery, Mr R G Labib, in an attempt to provide artists and interested members of the public with an opportunity to share space in which to work with empathetic others. Benefits available to members of the Foundation include 10% discount on all artists materials bought from the Arts Centre (fast becoming the most comprehensive stockist of arts materials in Brighton) and free admission to an annual members' exhibition to be held in the gallery attached to Muzart. As the yearly membership is at present only £5.00 working artists will appreciate that this sum could be recuperated by the saving on the buying of paints etc., if not by the sale of work during the group's exhibitions. Anyone interested in joining the Foundation is encouraged to call or telephone the Arts Centre between the hours of 9am and 5.30pm Monday to Saturday and ask for an application form. Meetings are held on Thursday evenings at 6.30pm at the Arts Centre. Full address: 12 York Place, Brighton, BN1 4GU. Tel:608232. Activities already discussed for commencement at the Arts Centre include painting, life drawing, wood carving, pottery, photography, block printing and sculpture.

OUT OF

Iranski (or thereabouts)
they fly free…freed…free!

to be encircled
by too much food
too many
political views

under this rich weight
they'll be imprisoned
for life!

John

Issue 1 of *Rubicon*, 1981.

SchNEWS 1994

This much-loved local alternative paper mocked prevailing consumer culture through satirical illustrations and cynical reporting. There is much to say about the worthiness of *SchNEWS* and how much it deserves its own chapter. It deserves a star on the alt-press boulevard although its debut is a bit late for the mimeograph scene and possibly unaware of the Brighton radical press tradition before it. The title still leaves us too early and is no longer published.

Notes

1 George Lakoff, *Moral Politics.*
2 Timothy Carder, *The Encyclopaedia of Brighton.*
3 Ibid.
4 Ibid.
5 John Amery was indicted after the war for treason. Davy Jones went on to edit *Fly* magazine, stand for parliament for the Green Party in Brighton Kemptown in 2015, and chair the Brighton Yoga Festival and Foundation.
6 *The Mole*, 1969.
7 https://unbound.com/boundless/2018/09/11/more-than-a-bookshop.
8 Ibid.
9 John Noyce and Francis Jarman (eds.), *Alternative Brighton*, 1973, p. 62.
10 Ibid. p. 6.
11 Ibid. p. 11.
12 http://revealdigital.com/independent-voices.
13 http://www.generalistarchive.co.uk.
14 https://blogs.brighton.ac.uk/radicalpress.
15 Ibid.
16 Ibid.
17 Ibid.
18 Ibid.

SchNEWS Stall at Boomtown Festival, 2010 by Grim23.

Queen's Park west, 2019
by Evlynn Sharp.

MUSIC

chapter 3

Hannah Smith

BRIGHTON IS A SPACE FOR ALTERNATIVE MUSIC of all genres to thrive, and an inclusive city in which many diverse performers and audiences can happily co-exist and experiment with their musical tastes. Jessica Kitt notes: "Brighton has long been a space for alternative musical subcultures, from the punks, mods and rockers, indie and rock, reggae, ska, hip hop, to name but a few."[1] One Brightonian recalls the diversity of the local music scene:

> In the early 80s the underground music scene was mostly centred around The Basement (under the art college). I played records between the bands there; saw U2 on the 'Boy' tour, Killing Joke when they set fire to the ceiling… There weren't many big venues then but we also had the Alhambra (now the Thistle Hotel), with local bands like The Midnight Lemon Boys and The Piranhas. The Pedestrian Arms (now The Foundry) put bands on but most people with funny hair were banned. […] Jenkinsons on the seafront (now the Odeon/Oceana) had bands like The Bunnymen and Teardrop Explodes […].[2]

Ballrooms, Birthdays and the Bourgeoisie

It is somewhat ironic that Brighton's dance scenes began with very formal and conventional culture of Grand Balls. High society visitors would congregate to eat, dance and exhibit their wealth during the 1700s. The enormous success,

35

The Piranhas performing at The Alhambra, 1978 by Peter Chrisp.

The Alhambra, 1911. Royal Pavilion & Museums.

The Starbeats at the Pedestrian Arms,
Foundry Street, c.1980s by Peter Chrisp.

grandeur and socialite reputation of these dances was further heightened by the frequent appearances of the Prince of Wales, who had developed a soft spot for Brighton from 1783 onwards. The aristocratic opulence of these events reached a regal climax in 1807 when a birthday ball was held at the Castle Inn for the Prince. Yet by the 1850s, these ostentatious events were in decline.

Over time the demand for socialising in musical settings transitioned into the frequenting of dance halls. Appealing to the lower and middle classes, venues such as The Regent in Queen's Road and Sherry's on West Street provided spaces in which young people could test out the new dance styles that had migrated over from America. Many local residents recall the ways in which dance halls provided alternative spaces for young people to express themselves. One woman recalls the solace she found in dancing: "It was a very difficult time for girls like myself who had never had a chance to be a teenager, because of the war. One day you were attending school, the next out to work, wearing grown-up clothes – some of them my mother's. There were no teenage clubs or any young activities, so Milly and I went dancing instead."[3] Another recollects how dance venues provided an interesting form of employment:

> ' When my mother lost her job on the trams she had to find another job to help support us. She was a marvellous dancer and she took a job in a dance hall in Gloucester Place as a dance hostess. When a man came in without a partner they could approach a hostess. They paid 4d a dance and she received a ticket for every dance she had. ' [4]

Illustration of the Assembly Rooms of the Castle Inn, Brighton, c. early 1800s. Royal Pavilion & Museums.

In the 1970s Sherry's Dixieland Showbar in West Street was a pioneer of disco dancing competitions, 1979 by Barry Pitman.

Dancing The Night Away at The Regent and Sherry's

The Regent Dance Hall was built on top of the arched roof of The Regent Cinema and opened in December 1923. The interior was dripping with art-deco influence with a zigzag design and coloured lights covering the walls. Kit Gosden remembers the novel fantasy of the space: "You went up in the lift and as soon as the lift doors opened you were in another world."[5] Iris Churcher firmly agrees: "The atmosphere there was beyond this world [...] Sometimes you'd just stand there, like you'd see in the movies, just standing there listening to the music because it was your favourite."[6]

Though many used the dance hall to meet and impress potential romantic partners, the venue had a fan base that also included local families, groups of friends and older residents. The Regent finally closed due to shifts in cultural interests, but the alternative legacy of the dance hall was acknowledged by Denys O'Loughlin who, after purchasing Chatfields, named it The New Regent. His son Terry recalls: "We had young hopefuls like U2, Madness, X-Ray Specs, XTC, and the Buzzcocks etc. performing weekly."[7] The bar "which promoted new wave bands, later to become punk bands"[8] illustrated the fluctuating musical tastes of the time whilst acknowledging the nuanced musical history it was born into.

The Regent's only real dance-hall rival was Sherry's, which opened in August 1919 and shared a very similar historical trajectory. The venue was "licensed, where you could sit at the tables in the balcony and watch the dancing."[9] Yet though the hall was initially designed to appeal to the bourgeoisie, as demonstrated by a pricey entry fee (four to five shillings!), the prices rapidly dropped and by the 1960s Sherry's became overshadowed by criminal activity. This nefarious reputation came hand in hand with its 1969 renovation from dance hall to nightclub, Sherry's Dixieland Bar, and adjoining amusement arcade, The Crystal Rooms. Gill Ditch recalls her student nights spent in the club:

The Richmond Bar

The burgeoning local rock and pop scene of the 1960s that swallowed up Sherry's was a booming presence in many other local venues. Found at 33 Richmond Place, The Richmond bar had metamorphosed from 1839 from inn to hotel to pub, which proved to be "a popular spot for jazz bands as far back as the 1950s."[11] By the early 1960s, it regularly held Sunday night dances on the top floor. As music tastes transitioned throughout the decade, so did The Richmond's performers: "evenings were featuring Blues and soul music [...] Mr Bob Harding, the Chimes, The Giants and the sapphires were some of the artists found playing here."[12]

The clientele included both unsuspecting visitors and dedicated locals, and notorious Brighton posses The Teddy Boys and Rockers "threw parties in the basement."[13] By the early 1980s, the venue's popularity and distinctive reputation led to the owners of The Zap Club to approach the bar. In 1983, Zap officially relocated to the upstairs of The Richmond, drawing in even larger crowds and generating great buzz in the alternative music scene. The Richmond pub encouraged a constant stream of unorthodox arts events, performances and art exhibitions:

The Richmond's reasonable capacity (200+) combined with the intimate and inclusive atmosphere made it a hot spot for touring Rock musicians throughout the 1980s and 90s. Many remember "The Stone Roses pack[ing] it out in 1988" and allegedly "Blur and Nirvana both played early gigs there."[15] The pub's dedication to upcoming music led to another rebranding in the 1990s to The Pressure Point Club. Rave music became the

Front of The Richmond bar, 2019 by Evlynn Sharp.

soundtrack to this new lease of life and its intake of dedicated visitors. The Pressure Point participated in the "first round of The Great Escape"[16] as well as welcoming local bands of all genres until 2008, when it finally shut down.

The Hungry Years

Similar to the devoted fan base The Richmond had acquired, The Hungry Years on Marine Parade gained eminence for its commitment to unconventional music. Given the arguable title "Brighton's oldest nightclub", the building was "first opened by ex-model Daphne Berry in 1973 after an £80,000 facelift."[17] The opening night was a celebration of jazz, as "800 people crowded the dance floor in the 1930s-themed venue to listen to [...] Bill le Sage, and the next night they came again to hear the Bee-Bop Preservation Society."[18] This family-run club, which had been purchased by John and Pepa Christoforou alongside the adjoining restaurant and pub in 1976, was sold on to Bass at the turn of the century and subsequently fizzled out, ending a legacy of wild nights on the seafront.[19]

Folk Music and The Stanford Arms

The inclusive nature of Brighton's alternative cultural landscape meant that there were sites specialising in all genres of music dotted around the city. Though the loud and radical punk and rock scene quickly gained prestige, other styles of music such as folk were also blossoming locally. In *Alternative Brighton*, the characteristics of a community folk venue are outlined in detail:

> The typical folk club is a room above a pub and "Club" is something of a misnomer, because although those who pay a membership fee are entitled to reduced admission, anyone is welcome to come along. Usually about 25p to get in. The local clubs will generally have a guest artist 3 weeks out of 4, with the other being a local singers' night, or a "Come-All-Ye". [20]

Many of the venues that revived Brighton and Hove's folk music scene were located in the London Road Station area from the mid 1960s-80s. Johnie Winch's Country and Gospel Club began at North Street's pub The Heart and Hand in 1962 and moved to The Stanford Arms at Preston Circus due to increasing demand.[21] The visitors and performers were intimate friends and contacts of Winches: "Wizz Jones, Bert Jansch, Johnny Duncan, Long John Baldry, Levee Breakers with Bev Martyn, Tom Paley, Mike Seeger and many more […]."[22] Tim Broadbent nostalgically recalls his teenage evenings spent at The Stanford as "nothing short of magical."[23] He remembers his favourite performances:

The Heart & Hand, 2019 by Evlynn Sharp.

> Too many names to mention but Miles Wootton, Johnie Winch (with whom I enjoyed many months touring in Germany), Rod Machling, Spud Taylor, Brian Golbey often rounded off the evening AFTER the guest spots and the ambiance was nothing short of electric with everyone singing – and simply enjoying a great night out. [24]

The club went through a number of names across the decade: under the new management of Jim Marshall in 1965 the musical group was changed to Brighton Singers Club and then later changed again to The Sunday Club. By the mid 70s, the group were seeking another location for performances and found a new home in The Springfield Hotel, just a stone's throw away from The Stanford. This hotel overlooking the neighbouring train tracks "was to remain [the club's] venue until 30 September 1984."[25] The convenient location for attendees travelling in from neighbouring towns such as Lewes ensured that the folk revival was not limited to locals living in the immediate vicinity but also included fans from across the whole of Sussex.

The bi-weekly folk clubs were so familiar with and indebted to the nearby transportation that some of the club's resident singers began to incorporate the echoes of the trains into the background of their music. Popular and recurring performers included Malcolm and Julia Donaldson (now a best-selling children's author), Miles Wootton and Allan Taylor, Johnie Winch, Rod Machling, Brian Golbey, Jerry Jordan and Derek Lockwood.[26] Tucked away on the liminal outskirts of Brighton's bustling and oftentimes aggressively radical music scene, these passionate traditional music artists were quietly reigniting an alternative revolution for folk music.

Skulls and Street Punk at The Vault

The Punk movement of the late 70s was engulfing central Brighton. Openly disapproving of the folk music and hippie counterculture that was being nurtured in the outskirts of the city, local punk rockers sought out a venue to express their radical opinions. They decided that the underground space below former the Presbyterian Church, The Brighthelm Centre, was to be their stomping ground. The ironic pairing of the location and its new residents might appear to undermine the Punks' rejection of institutionalised establishments, but maybe the extreme mismatch of the setting ultimately reaffirmed the anarchical disobedience that lay at the heart of the movement.

A looming presence on North Road, The Brighthelm Centre is now a United Reformed Christian Church and a popular community space, but its unassuming façade hides the secrets of a tempestuous history. Named The Vault, the punk rehearsal and gig space was "a 150-year-old crypt with a series of intact tombs"[27] that lay underneath what at the time was the Brighton Resource Centre. Initially, the live music crypt "hosted gigs and must have been the nearest thing to the Liverpool Cavern Brighton is ever likely to see. Many bands played on the makeshift stage in the early days."[28]

Quickly, the alternative venue was "developed into rehearsal spaces constructed by the bands themselves, who built doorways and walls in front of the old burial chambers for individual rehearsal rooms."[29] The unmonitored DIY generated wider issues of security for bands, with many of the arched rooms forced to have "reinforced steel doors to try to stem the tide of constant break-ins."[30]

Bigger structural safety concerns were on the horizon for The Vault's alternative lodgers. The frequency and sheer volume of the music being performed created vibrations that began to damage and corrode the walls of the crypt. Combined with casual vandalism and the constant renovation for more working space, cracks appeared, which meant "bones and pieces of coffin belonging to the Huguenot refugees who had died of plague in the 1800s started to emerge from the walls."[31] It was rumoured that "more disrespectful members of the punk scene began removing skulls, bones and full coffins", with "the skull of a child […] found in a nearby phone box."[32]

The council quickly intervened and shut down the venue. Though the unorthodox sub-culture soon depleted in numbers through the late 1980s and

90s, their alternative legacy does still live on in the recesses of Brighton. Abigail Young notes the "small but significant group of aging punk rockers in Brighton […] many of which can be found at the members-only Cowley Club on London Road", endeavouring to keep the anarchic fire lit.[33]

The Art College Basement: Brighton's Radical Rabbit Warren

Another underground venue that thrived during the culturally experimental 1970s and 80s was The Art College Basement. Found on "the lower ground floor of the rambling Glenside Annexe immediately adjacent to the main College of Art building in Grand Parade",[34] The Basement was filled with eccentric and radical students desperate to experiment. Much like the claustrophobic Vault, the venue had a central location and was a "[…] dark, dingy, wet-floored, low-ceilinged series of interconnecting spaces."[35]

It was this distinctive alternative atmosphere that drew students away from traditional music nights arranged by the other university campus'. The nonconformist fashion, music and politics of its visitors ensured The Basement became a "became a highly popular venue with […] all the stylistic idiosyncrasies and vivacity associated with art school life."[36] Often referred to as a "local rite of passage" the space also provided income to its Student Union owners.[37]

Embraced by the student community as a bar, a club, a performance area, rehearsal space and general hub of unconventional counterculture, The Basement provided publicity for bands new to the music scene. These included U2, Echo & the Bunnymen, New Order and The Levellers. Basement organiser and savvy graphics student Addison Cresswell personally "oversaw the marked transition away from The Basement's Friday Night Club predilection for Heavy Metal music towards more cutting edge Punk and New Wave developments."[38]

As finances began to dwindle, Cresswell worked alongside fellow student Anthony Wilson to attempt to maximise The Basement's profits by creating novelty nights and securing popular performers. These fleeting club nights included Hot Club, a Women Only evening and The Wardrobe Club where guests entered through a large clothes cupboard. Yet the physical limitations of the space created logistical problems:

> ❛The Basement Club was still a dark, labyrinthine, often wet-floored, cramped space with a safety limit of 200. The makeshift stage was constructed from ply-board supported on either beer crates or wooden pallets, but couldn't be built too high as the ceiling was so low.❜ [39]

Equipment was limited and worn out. When questioned by U2's Bono about band lighting pre-performance, Cresswell "pointed to two spotlights – one red and one white, purchased from B&Q – and told him that the white was for him and the red for the band."[40] The venue's celebration of the unconventional inspired the creation and development of other cultural ventures across Brighton and Hove. Doorman Dave Reeves "future co-founder and co-director of the Zap"[41] later expanded on The Basement's experimental ethos with the birth of his infamous seaside club. Though economically unstable, The Basement – well up until its closure in 1996 – continued to provide a home for anyone in the community who felt different or misunderstood.

Gay Clubs and Siren

Another style of venue that was contributing to the eclectic musical scene of 1970s and 80s Brighton were Gay Clubs. The local community had an ever-increasing list of inclusive spaces that celebrated LGBTQ+ culture. In *Daring Hearts*, contributor Dennis recalls how Gay Clubs evolved through the second half of the twentieth century:

> I remember coming down from Bradford and apart from The Spotted Dog and Terry's Bar, The Greyhound was gay; little bar at The Greyhound, presided over by a succession of old queans but that was a bit of an elephants' graveyard really. And the 42 Club was the only gay club in the fifties. [...] And then Ray opened another one up Middle Street called the Variety Club, which is where the school is now. [...] And then a whole profusion of gay clubs just sprang up, all small ones. There was the Regency Club in Regency Square, there was the Queen of Clubs, which Ray opened in Bedford Square, and then, of course, there was the Curtain Club. [...] you got all age groups there; they weren't all old but at the same time, everybody sort of behaved themselves and kept a low profile and it wasn't outrageous. It started to liven up towards the end of the sixties, when everything else started to loosen up, when things had got gay and we had got flower power. Well, of course, they had it down here with a vengeance as you can imagine they would. And Ray Bishop took the Heart and Hand in Ship Street and that became very gay indeed, a sort of Aquarium of its day. And then he took the Curtain Club and made that very gay and there was a disco put in with disco lights and the whole place started to swing. [42]

Similarly, Grant recalls his favourite local club The Regina on North Street, an alternative space that was both welcoming and unashamedly ostentatious:

> [...] when I went in I was extremely impressed because it had a very grand entrance up a magnificent flight of stairs. The proverbial flight of stairs you see in pantomimes, with Dames coming down. And when we got there I must admit it was breathtaking. It was a beautiful carpet, the whole length of the room was a bar, completely mirrored at the back, with the most beautiful crystal chandeliers you've ever seen in your life. A very nice grand piano in the window. Seats all round the wall, it was so unusual, all the seats were black velvet. The bar was white plastic on top, but cushioned black velvet, the front of it. Everything else was gold, so the whole thing was black and gold. It just hit you as being black and gold. It was very ornate. Anyway we went in, and the owner made us very welcome, he'd got some canned music on. My friend said, 'You've got a nice big piano, haven't you got a pianist? My friend here plays the piano, he'll play for you.' And that's how it started. The music had to be cover for

Siren Band.

conversation. It wasn't to be listened to. Although if someone wanted to convey something to someone else without going up and saying it, they would ask me to play whatever it was. [43]

By the 1980s a handful of club nights refreshed the LGBTQ+ music scene in Brighton, creating more diversity. One-nighter Club Shame held at The Zap Club drew in a large raving audience from London. Monthly rave night Wild Fruit followed suit in 1992

with similar levels of popularity. The nightclub Revenge was born in 1991: with its buzzing atmosphere, cheap drinks and alternative playlists, it is popular to this day. Contributing to the music and dance scene were:

'London clubs such as Popstars and Crash [that] were running one-nighters in the City and a number of new venues [that] had joined the older establishments around St James's Street, making the area truly a Gay Village. The year

2000 also saw the first full-time bar for lesbians open in Brighton.' [44]

One band that emerged from Brighton's eclectic musical atmosphere of the 70s and 80s was lesbian feminist punk band Siren. Their members include Jane Boston on guitar and vocals, Tash Fairbanks on bass guitar, Deb Trethewey on drums, Jude Winter on synthesizer and keyboards, and Emilia Ballardini on vocals.[45] These women identify their ethos as "pushing the boundaries as women in a male music world, with our own politically radical songs and punchy, eclectic style."[46] Their culturally relevant music addresses politics and other subjects "from a lesbian feminist perspective."[47] The band members recall their rise in popularity:

'We produced two albums in the 80s, *Siren in Queer Street* and *Siren Plays* and toured as a band and a theatre company throughout the UK and in Holland, Belgium, Germany, Switzerland and the USA. Four of Siren members also played in the Brighton band, Bright Girls. It was the heady days of the Women's Movement, with thousands marching through the UK demanding our right to self-determination. It was during this ten-year period of questioning and challenging, mixed in with a dose of the 'let's have a go' punk attitude that Siren toured and performed.' [48]

Though the band members temporarily went their own ways, in 2014 Siren reformed and are continuing their punk-fuelled legacy with more songwriting and performances in local venues. The five women openly reflect on their style and new content: "Naturally our perspective is still strongly feminist and politically radical […but] We're also now challenging the stereotype of aging, being living proof that older women can still pack out a venue with our alternative rock songs."[49] In a 2018 review published in *Gscene*, music critic Ray A J comments on the raw power that Siren captured in their live performance at Brighton venue The Brunswick:

'[Siren] began bleeding the raw, kick-ass anarchism that their older music was all about – only now packaged up in a beautifully refined style of classic rock […] Although the politics was practically bubbling in hot fury throughout their performance that night, their wonderful sense of humour and light tales of love, were injected into each song too, just to keep it all from spilling too far into darkness.' [50]

(opposite page) Door surround, Brighton, 2019 by Evlynn Sharp.

Notes

1 Jessica Kitt, 'From the "Mod" to the Modern: The Lowdown on Brighton's Music Scene', *Picture Britain*.

2 David Courtney, Allan Fowler, Damian Harris, James Kendall and The Perv, 'Brighton since the 60s', *The Brighton Source*.

3 Barbara Chapman, *Boxing Day Baby* (Brighton: QueenSpark Books, 1994).

4 Various, *Blighty Brighton* (Brighton: QueenSpark Books, 1991).

5 'Remember the Regent', *Sparchives, Queen's Park News*, Spring 81.

6 Ibid.

7 Terry O'Loughlin, 'Regent Dance Hall', *My Brighton and Hove*.

8 'Regent Dance Hall'.

9 Marjory Batchelor, *A Life Behind Bars* (Brighton: QueenSpark Books, 1999).

10 Gill Ditch, contributor.

11 Bailey, Ben, 'The Richmond Returns', *The Brighton Source*.

12 Ibid.

13 Ibid.

14 Ibid.

15 Ibid.

16 Ibid.

17 'End of an era for "gatherers"', *The Argus*, 3 July 2000.

18 Ibid.

19 Ibid.

20 John Noyce and Francis Jarman, *Alternative Brighton* (Brighton: Unicorn Bookshop Publications, 1973), p. 93.

21 'London Road Station as an Asset', *The Round Hill Society*, http://www.roundhill.org.uk.

22 Ibid.

23 Tim Broadbent, 'Circus Circus, 2 Preston Road – previously Stanford Arms', *My Brighton and Hove*.

24 Ibid.

25 'London Road Station'.

26 Ibid.

27 'From the "Mod" to the Modern'.

28 https://www.punkbrighton.co.uk/vaultn.html.

29 'From the "Mod" to the Modern'.

30 https://www.punkbrighton.co.uk/vaultn.html.

31 'From the "Mod" to the Modern'.

32 https://www.punkbrighton.co.uk/vaultn.html.

33 'From the "Mod" to the Modern'.

34 Jonathan M. Woodham, 'The 'Art College' Basement: some recollections', *University of Brighton*.

35 Ibid.

36 Ibid.

37 Ibid.

38 Ibid.

39 Ibid.

40 Ibid.

41 Ibid.

42 Peter Dennis, Beccie Mannall and Linda Pointing, *Daring Hearts* (Brighton: QueenSpark Books in collaboration with Brighton Ourstory, 1992), p. 71.

43 Ibid. p. 63.

44 http://www.brightonourstory.co.uk.

45 Siren, contributor.

46 Ibid.

47 Ibid.

48 Ibid.

49 Ibid.

50 A-J, Ray, 'Interview: Siren – "They're pushing the boundaries again."', *Gscene*.

the Zap Club
opens
its doors!

chapter 4

Gill Ditch

EACH GENERATION SEEMS TO FIND THE SPACES they like to frequent whether it be eating out, dancing or listening to music. Some of these places lend themselves to the creation of special memories; they are different, they push boundaries and become the place to go. One such place in Brighton that epitomised being different in the early 1980s was the Zap Club.

History of the Zap Club

> ' The whole concept of Zap grew out of a natural meeting of minds. Neil Butler, Pat Butler and Dave Reeves had all been students at Brighton College of Education and Sussex University in the early 1970s and had been involved in putting on a range of social events. ' [1]

The founders and others associated with Zap had been involved in a range of initiatives such as the Contemporary Arts Festivals of the later 1970s (described in Chapter Seven). Coming together to create the Zap concept was almost inevitable:

> ' By the early 1980s Brighton was awash with music and performance. Outlandish clothes and eccentricity were commonplace and there was a generosity towards new ideas and new approaches. Nearly all the elements that were to provide the platform for the Zap were in place. "We scraped together all the money we could find, hired the basement of the New Oriental Hotel, and devised a programme. ' IAN SMITH [2]

Founding members of the Zap Club, 1985 by Brighton *Evening Argus*.

'The arrival of the Zap was welcome as it provided a space for performance, cabaret as well as music. Two of the directors had been fellow students from teacher training days; we were all part of the baby boomer generation born into the cultural revolution of the 60s. It is no surprise Neil and Dave were part of the movement to create places in Brighton where artists and performances could flourish. A night out at the Zap was an experience as you never knew who you would meet there; in my memory it embodies the spirit of Brighton.' GILL DITCH

Founding Members

' The early Zap Club was built as a brand – a night out that you could trust. A brand that would expose you to thought-provoking and sometimes worrying art, programmed alongside anarchic, iconoclastic entertainment. From 1982-84 around 200 people came every week to the New Oriental Hotel, then the Escape, and finally the Richmond for the Zap experience. Zap was always about ideas and ideology. Imagine a place of visionaries and iconoclasts, tricksters and dreamers. Where artists think of their audience and audiences demand to be challenged and provoked. Zap was always about providing alternatives to the established arts economy. ' [3]

Development of the Club

The Zap became ever more popular and the increased numbers meant the founders had to consider a larger venue:

Neil Butler, 1989 by Mark Power.

'The Zap Club was an experiment. Everyone who creates a real club is making a place that doesn't exist – a space they want to go to. We wanted to see visionary artists inspire us. We wanted to be challenged by new vocabularies and subversive thoughts. We wanted a great night out we would remember and could think about. And we had found the right place to do it. Brighton.'
NEIL BUTLER, ZAP FOUNDER[5]

The move to the Arches on the Seafront was an inspired move, as it attracted more people to the area and prompted additional developments nearby:

'Audiences grew, and the key difference in attitude that evolved was that people came to a Zap Club Night, not necessarily to see a headliner or favourite act. The billing was so esoteric, punters probably wouldn't have heard of most of the artists anyway. The point was that everything and everybody – acts, audience and atmosphere – could be fresh and fascinating when juxtaposed with unlikely partners. Stalwarts at the Royal Escape included everyone from Lynn Thomas and Pete McCarthy, to Topo the Mime, J.J. Waller, John Hegley and most of the Liverpool Poets.' IAN SMITH[4]

'Three and a half years after the idea was first conceived, the Zap Club got a permanent home in two (191/193 Kings Rd) arches on 1 November 1984. The arches were converted by architect Anthony Browne, with staff and artists volunteering labour, from digging foundations alongside the real builders to painting the damp walls with endless coats of waterproofing. On its opening, the Zap was marketed to members as a club for artists, run by artists who understand performers and their needs. The move to the seafront arches was a huge risk. Dave Reeves brought entrepreneurial business experience and a unique

Early Zap Club Flyer, 1983.

performing style. Angie Livingstone (now Goodchild) came with a background in catering and a love of fashion. And Pat Butler kept us (sometimes tenuously) attached to reality. Between us we mortgaged virtually everything we owned. The new Zap at the arches was built by friends, many of whom were artists or performers or firemen, and in at least one case – a builder. '[6]

Developing new talent

The Zap Club was the place for new talent to try out their acts and for more experienced acts to reach a new audience. It provided space for artists and performers to hone their skills. Acts such as The Pookies, The Pierrotters, The Wild Wigglers and Theatre of the Bleeding Obelisk all had an influence on the performance scene in Britain:

' The Zap Club provided an "Opportunity to contextualise practice in the mid 1980s for

The Pierrotters, by The West Pier, c.1987. From Dr. Tony Lidington, AKA Uncle Tacko! (from top to bottom: Sleazy Slacko, Nurse Wacko, Dirty Doctor Dacko, the Reverend Uncle Tacko!, Mister Macko).

students, local wannabes and future artistes, there was the pleasure of seeing 'established' performance/dance/alternative artists ... right on your Brighton doorstep: Rose English, Kathy Acker, Phil Jeck and his Turntable Orchestra, John Hegley and his glasses; alternative artistes, dance artistes; Laurie Booth, Lea Anderson and early Cholmondeleys. You name it. It was there. A roll-call for a future. The Zap flourished because there was an audience, an interest, and a thriving and ambitious community, and it gave artists, whether from Brighton or elsewhere, an opportunity to perform, practice their art, and ply their trade. **'** PROFESSOR LIZ AGGISS[8]

In addition, Ian Smith created the Tuesday Night platform:

'I wondered about the people who had aspirations to perform but perhaps not the chutzpah to face the increasingly cruel and cynical 'open spots' and 'gong shows' that were becoming the accepted routes to 'going professional'. The 'Tuesday Night Platform' was born. The chemistry required an unspoken

Zap Club arches, Brighton seafront by Ray Gibson.

Roger Ely.

shingle beach, and break their teeth on seaside rock. The Zap Club, when it opened in 1984 in its arch under King's Road, seemed dazzling and original, but in many ways was just another in a long line of moments when the sea came to the rescue of the town. Whatever its claims to novelty at the time, and, make no mistake, it was indeed daring and singular at its birth, it was one marker in a long history.' [10]

contract between the audience (mainly other aspirants) and the performers – "don't abuse the scene by over-running your five-minute spot, and we won't give you a hard time." **IAN SMITH** [9]

Other innovations included the introduction of Mini-festivals, which enabled the club to explore more controversial topics.

The seafront influence and the growth of the Zap Club

The seafront has always exerted an influence on visitors to Brighton. People were drawn to the seafront area to relax, promenade, eat ice cream and explore the entertainments on the piers:

' Squillions of tourists who have flocked ever since the railway made it a cheap day out in the 1840s, came to paddle, kiss each other quick on the

Zap Poster by Ian Miller.

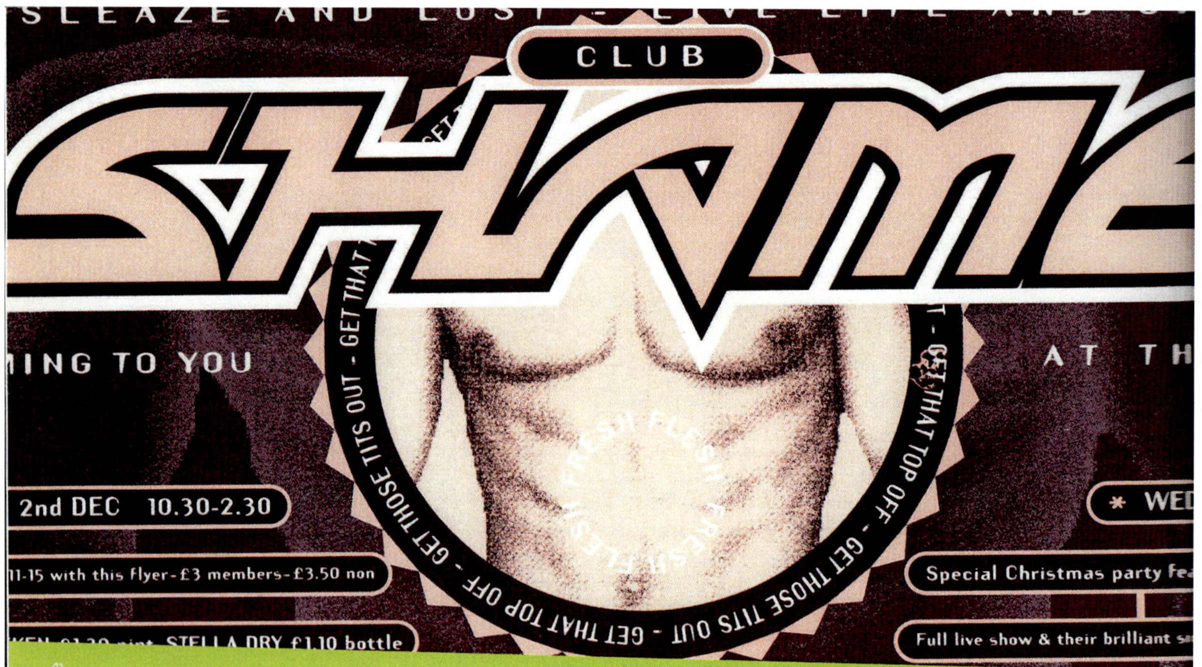

'Like so many businesses and organisations the Zap Club had to reinvent itself in order to adapt to change. It also opened its doors to an eclectic array of music styles from jazz and world music to unadulterated pop. As the eighties made way for the nineties, Zap was once again at the leading edge of a new cultural revolution: the burgeoning clubbing scene that spawned acid house, techno, trance and rave culture. Its club nights – from Frenzy and Coco Club to Club Shame and Pro-Techtion – not only put Brighton on the clubbing map, but they also became a catalyst for a unique experiment in mixing club culture and performance art.' [11]

Some were concerned about the use of the term 'Club Shame', and did not appreciate the Zap's ironic use of the word:

'Nevertheless, Shame would soon coax Brighton's fledgling gay club scene into a bold, fresh and more open world of dance-orientated gay clubbing nineties style. Shame soon gained national notoriety and saw clubbers travelling from across the UK to Brighton in unprecedented numbers to sample its infamous delights. There were even special coaches laid on for London visitors.' [12]

Zap, as a result of its range of specialist club nights, attracted an eclectic range of clubbers and followers, many of whom also performed at the club. It also actively marketed the venue to local people and complimentary memberships were given to the Nightingale Theatre Company, Riverside Studios and groups such as Luke Cresswell who, with Steve McNicholas, formed Yes/No People, were members of Pookiesnackenburger, and produced and directed Stomp, which featured at the Zap Club in 1990.

> **'In the early days, the grim and angry mid-eighties when Thatcherism had seemed to last a lifetime and south coast youth was rebelling in full eyeliner the Zap saved our lives by playing host not only to mega-stars like Marc Almond, but also to the Hairy Dog Club on Saturday at lunchtime.'**
> POLLY MARSHALL[13]

Zap Moving On

Like all long-running creative ventures, the Zap Club evolved:

> In the late 1980s the Zap Club changed in the space of a few weeks, as house music began to filter into the country and our DJ collective consciousness. Mostly the musical diet was funky classics – James Brown, Talking Heads, Soft Cell, Nina Simone. The Zap was like a time machine, it was at least a year ahead of other clubs and a test ground for fashion and music. It's impossible to overstate the importance of the Zap Club in that it helped to create the club/rave scene which took hold of Britain at the turn of the 1990s. [14]

> **'Zap was quite simply the best club experience of the time, gay or straight. I simply can't find the words to describe how important Club Shame was to the gay scene at that time, nor how much it contributed to the club scene in general. It was, certainly on this side of the Atlantic, very unusual at that time to find a gay club that attracted straight clubbers as well. Its importance and legacy stems from the fact that it wasn't just a breakthrough in gay liberation; it smashed through the glass ceiling.'** SIMON, REGULAR ZAP CLUBBER, LATE 80S AND EARLY 90S[15]

The Legacy of Zap

The Zap Club acted as a springboard for many initiatives and projects both nationally and internationally, and the legacy of this club should not be underestimated:

> It sought to promote high impact events beyond the club. Early manifestations included the Rose Street Carnival at the Edinburgh Festival

and Hogmanay Celebrations in Glasgow in 1987. In 1988 Zap had programmes at the South Bank Centre and was part of the creative team for Glasgow's year as European City of Culture. Zap Tents with their distinctive edgy programming had started appearing around the UK, and Zap began a short but explosive relationship producing the perfectly named Archaos Circus. On a more international front, in 1991 Zap Productions also organised a Japanese Festival (Matsuri – Japan in the Park) in Hyde Park, London. The Zap Tent, launched in the mid 1980s, also featured acts at festivals around Britain, ensuring that Zap's particular brand of innovation in the visual and performing arts reached the widest audiences.' [16]

Zap's importance to Brighton

'After thirteen years in its permanent home beneath King's Road, the original Zap Club was sold to Webb Kirby Ltd in November 1997. During its time it played host to an eclectic array of performers, artists and musicians including Julian Clary, Roger McGough, Rory Bremner, Edwin Collins, Mark Almond, Chemical Brothers, Sonic Youth, John Hegley, Forkbeard Fantasy, Blur, Paul Weller, Mark Steel, Stomp, Ali Farka Tourre and Eddie Izzard to name but a few. Since the demise of the Zap Club a different culture has developed within the Brighton arts community with organisations that provide artistic support and another kind of home such as Brighton Fringe Arts Productions, The Nightingale Theatre and South East Dance. The alternative Live Art /performance culture that had, through the Zap, an ad-hoc start in Brighton has now become a recognised part of the fabric of the community. It is significant that many of the Zap's innovatory ideas have since been successfully developed by others.' [17]

'The Zap was the start of something by the sea. As the channel always reminds us in Brighton, we live on the edge. And when the tide rolls in and out it always starts and ends somewhere new.' [18]

'In its simplest form, the Zap was a platform that moved out of the club into the street. It moved from playing with the chemistry of place, art and entertainment in an arch by the sea to commissioning work for clubs, fields, the street and shopping malls. Always exploring new economies and new partnerships that would keep artists free from institutions and exposed to an audience that hadn't been trained to a particular art form in a particular environment.' [19]

A timeline link that highlights the development of Zap's twenty-five years of innovation is available online. [20]

Notes

1 Woodham, JM, N Butler, R Ely, L Aggiss,
I Smith, S Fanshawe, S Thomas et al.,
ZAP: Twenty-Five Years of Innovation
(Brighton: QueensSpark Books, 2007).

2 Ibid.

3 Ibid.

4 Ibid.

5 Ibid.

6 Ibid.

7 Ibid.

8 Ibid.

9 Ibid.

10 Ibid.

11 Ibid.

12 Ibid.

13 Ibid.

14 Ibid.

15 Ibid.

16 Ibid.

17 Ibid.

18 Ibid.

19 Ibid.

20 https://www.mybrightonandhove.org.uk
(search 'zap')

Liz Aggiss in Grotesque
Dancer, 1986 by Billy Cowie.

FESTIVALS,
PERFORMANCE
& THEATRE

Children's Parade, first day of Brighton Festival, 2015 by Daren Holes.

chapter 5
Siobhán Laroche

PERFORMANCE, CREATIVE EXPRESSION AND engagement with culture in Brighton have long taken place in a range of different spaces beyond traditional venues – outdoors and even on the beach. As well as providing unique possibilities for the creators and performers themselves, unconventional and alternative spaces enable a wider audience to access culture and cultural experiences. Underlining the importance of artists "who think differently about engaging with audiences", Dave Reeves of Zap Productions points out the value of "recognis[ing] what audiences want" and how alternative venues allow audiences to "engage in a completely different way than they would do in a theatre or a conventional space." Reeves emphasises that engaging with culture "in an unconventional way" appeals "for a multitude of reasons … a big proportion of people don't go to the theatre at all", but "still like to engage with some sort of cultural experience", enjoying events like "the Children's Parade, Pride or Streets of Brighton."[1]

The Contemporary Festival of Arts: "An important impetus in the genesis of Brighton's alternative culture"[2]

In the late 1970s, Roger Ely and art school friends Neil Butler and Dave Reeves founded and organised the Brighton Contemporary Festival of Arts (1976-79). The first Festival:

> … embraced many venues across Brighton, including the Sallis Benney Theatre, the adjacent Norfolk Public House (now Hector's House) and The Basement [at the

Original Contemporary Festival of Arts poster, 1977.

Art College]. Performances at the latter included the Liverpool poet Adrian Henri, guitarist Andy Roberts, saxophonists Evan Parker and Lol Coxhill, the Mike Osborne Quintet, the George Khan Quartet *Mirage*, and performance artists Stuart Brisley, Diz Willis, and Kevin Atherton. A similarly adventurous line-up infused subsequent Festivals and did much to enhance the cultural horizons of the town.' [3]

Roger Ely, the Festival programmer, reflects on the Festival's development:

' Neil and I wanted the 1977 Brighton Contemporary Arts Festival to introduce the diverse work of these emergent and established artists to the people: "A showcase of contemporary performing art previously unavailable in Brighton and to involve the community by presenting free and publicly available events that will reinforce their efficacy in society."

We prioritised these site-specific outside events over the consideration of any financial gain, because we saw them as being the most important element in kick-starting creative activity in Brighton. There were pockets of alternative culture surviving from the 1960s, particularly the Public House Book Shop (who we were to work closely with in producing festivals and events in 1978 and 1979), but most had moved on.

When we presented the first series of events in 1976 and the first Festival proper the following year, people had had very little experience of this diverse, indefinable area of creativity. There were few venues supporting this type of work. We distributed publicity far and wide, attracting supporters and artists from all over the UK [...] We felt that a festival of this kind could help address this drain of artists abroad and facilitate the social and political change needed in the country. By centring the festival at the Polytechnic, we set it up as an example of what other educational establishments and student unions could do.' [4]

IOU Theatre Company performing on Brighton beach at Brighton Contemporary Festival of Arts, 1977 by Mike Laye.

Performer and artist Ian Smith arrived in Brighton aged 19 in 1978 when the Contemporary Festival of Arts was developing. He recalls being "ready to jump into the newly formed 'Expressive Arts' course" and "to eat up any opportunity thrown at [him]":

> ... the [Festival's] programme included the prime movers of the British alternative scene, who were creeping out of agitprop street theatre and delighting in subverting the status quo indoors, outdoors, and more often than not, in the pub. By offering my services as a leafleteer, sandwich-board wearer, etc., I got to hang out with the likes of Ian Hinchliffe, Dave Stephens, Rob Conn, Jeff Nuttall, Roland Miller and Shirley Cameron, Lol Coxhill and of course Roger Ely.
>
> Seeing these madmen and women at their best and worst, and tentatively joining in with a few endurance performances of my own, it was encouraging to encounter grizzled grown-ups who thought presenting weirdness a perfectly valid lifestyle. One particular solo performer (the late) Bob Carroll – explaining the entire universe via the life cycle of a salmon just by waving his arms around and declaiming in a room above a pub – provided an iconic standard for everybody that witnessed it. [6]

1979, the year following Ian Smith's arrival, proved to be a landmark year in the Festival's development. Music, theatre, film, video and performance art events took place in locations across the city, including Brighton Polytechnic and Grand Parade. The programme also featured exhibitions and installations, drama, mime and music workshops and street theatre, dance and musical performances. Acts included the People Show, IOU Theatre Co., the Feminist Improvising Group, sound poetry group Konkrete Kantikle, Afro-Caribbean steel band/ pantomime/ dance group Steel 'n' Skin Community Arts, Viv Stanshall, Ivor Cutler and Spirits Rejoice jazz group. Many local performers took part in the "Festival '79", including Nicky & The Dots, Last Resort Theatre Co., Brighton Community Arts Workshop and film-makers Rob Gawthrop and Tony Sinden.

The Festival was now "one of the most extensive contemporary arts festivals in Britain."[7] Roger Ely recalls:

> By the time of Festival '79 many had "joined the party." By then the music press, particularly *NME*, fanzines and the emergence of a performance art press (*Performance* magazine and *PS Primary*

Mural on seafront during Brighton Festival, 1984 by Peter Chrisp.

Sources) along with punk/new wave distributors and companies like Rough Trade had emerged [...] In Brighton there was a growth of bands and performers [...] Festival '79 was different from the preceding years' events, in that the local arts and music scene had developed strongly over the two years since the first festival, and this was reflected in the programming. Many of the events were free and took place outside and over extended time periods (from hours to days). There was the continued practice of having workshops and lectures by visiting artists – encouraging local artists and introducing new ideas and skills. There was a large video and film

"Festival '79" was also the final Contemporary Festival of Arts. Even though the Festival only ran for a few years, its contribution to Brighton's alternative cultural history was a significant one.

Brighton Festival and Brighton Fringe

One of the city's most important cultural events is the annual Brighton Festival, which is enjoyed by Brightonians and visitors from across the world alike. Established in 1967, Brighton Festival is now the largest arts festival in England, seeing the city of Brighton and Hove transformed into a platform for culture for the whole month of May. The Festival has established Brighton as a "city on the edge"[9], cementing its reputation as a cultural hub of global significance for fresh, unconventional and alternative local and international talent.

The Festival's first director, Ian Hunter, was "explicitly both international and *avant garde*, new and experimental in his ambitions."[10] The first Festival already featured the exciting, unique and bizarre. The programme included a kinetic labyrinth on the West Pier, an attempt to paint the sea red, Concrete Poetry and the Destruction of Hideous Objects – a huge bonfire of old furniture and ugly art on Brighton beach.[11]

During the early Festivals, events centred around Brighton Polytechnic, Brighton Municipal Art Gallery and the Theatre Royal, but the idea of using alternative spaces was already emerging. There were outdoor artistic displays, including a continuous doodle running along the seafront between the Palace and West Piers.[12] Gavin Henderson's directorship, from 1984 to 1994, saw the festival continue to expand in size and scope, as well as duration. The Children's Parade began in 1985 and literature, jazz, international theatre and dance events also became part of the Festival.[13] As the Festival grew, international comedy and street performances featured more regularly in the programme.[14]

The Zap Club at the Brighton Festival

The Festival also gave the Zap Club the opportunity to work on larger scale projects beyond its own venue. It established its own Zap Tent in a derelict town-centre car park: "this big top, packed with an extremely accessible programme, was immensely popular with the great unwashed of Brighton who seldom attended "official" festival events."[15]

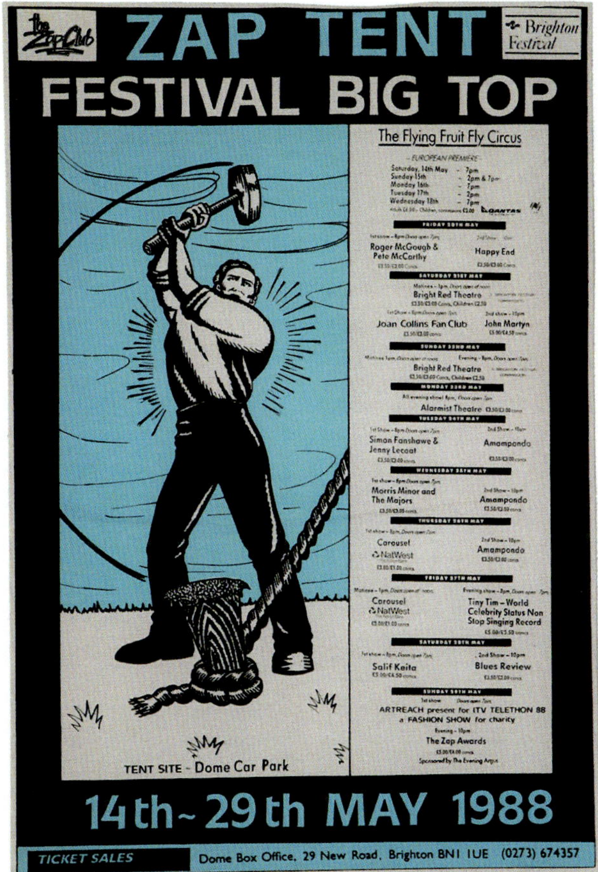

The Zap Tent poster, 1988. [The Zap Tent became a major feature of Brighton's annual May festival.]

it proved such a soaraway success that the organisers decided to expand and take the same mix of entertainment on the road. *

YORKSHIRE POST ON YORK FESTIVAL 1988[16]

The Zap was also involved in creating The Arts Unit, which provided "a means of finally developing a Brighton-based production and promotional team for the Festival, as well as being a focus for year-round creative activity." This made it "a crucial foundation at a time when the arts began to blossom in Brighton."[17] In its venue in a shop opposite The Corn Exchange, the Arts Unit served as:

> ... a year-round promotional centre for all the various artistic endeavours, galleries, pub theatre and jazz clubs. With it came a budget for grant aid, which in turn allocated funding to the Zap, and also established the basis for recruiting a new community arts initiative. This came to life as Same Sky and kick-started a theatre company called Bright Red out of which grew the busking troupe The Pierrotters.[18]

In this way, "the Festival also acted as a lobbying force to establish a more enlightened policy for arts support with Brighton's local authority (until 1986, a Conservative-run council)."[19]

Before becoming established in its own venue, the Zap produced Brighton Festival events at the Pavilion and Sallis Benney theatres. The Zap played a key role in taking culture to alternative and more accessible venues to "shift the axis" and "break loose from the assumption that the Dome/Royal Pavilion estate was [the Festival's] only base." 1985 saw the Zap, now establishing itself in its new location, collaborating in a range of acts at the club, with artists in residence such as Roland Miller and Rose English, creating installations and living sculpture. The Zap also worked with the Industrial and Domestic Theatre Contractors on their installation under the West Pier. By 1986, the Zap was, in Gavin Henderson's words "in full swing, functioning as a nightly social centre and alternative Festival club."[20]

Streets of Brighton Festival

As the Festival grew, street performances also became increasingly prevalent. These events, which were free and accessible to all, termed "a people's art form" by Dave Reeves,[21] were at the centre of the Streets of Brighton Festival. Launched during Brighton Festival 1995, Streets of Brighton soon developed into one of the UK's largest and most vibrant street festivals as well as an important feature of the Brighton Festival programme. From 1997, it also featured the annual National Street Arts Meeting, which served as "a platform for artists, producers, arts officers, programmers and funders to meet and debate current street arts issues."[22]

Jane McMorrow, Brighton Festival Programmer from 2001 to 2008, recalls her memories of Streets of Brighton Festival 2006:

> It is 12 May 2006 and I am tearing along to get to a production meeting at the Brighton Festival offices. I am on my way through Pavilion

World Record Attempt at Apathy, Comic Character Creations, Streets of Brighton, 2006 by Ray Gibson.

Gardens and am stopped dead in my tracks by a large maze that overnight has appeared in the middle of the Gardens. A maze? It looks like it has always been there! I am not the only person who is stopping to take a look: there are many curious people around. It's not open yet. When will I be able to take a look inside? It is the second weekend of Brighton Festival and this is Streets of Brighton, a weekend when residents of Brighton

Sticky **by Improbable Theatre, Streets of Brighton, 2002 by Alan McAteer.**

and Hove have come to expect the unexpected but it still catches you out!

A few hours later I return to Pavilion Gardens to see a queue of people waiting to get the opportunity. The dotmaze *Get Lost* is created by street art supremos dotComedy and represents just one of the many varied and thrilling companies that Zap Art has brought to Brighton Festival for Streets of Brighton over the years. And dotComedy, produced by Zap Art, have once again done the thing they do so well: they have transformed a familiar space into something totally magical.❜ [23]

As the festival developed, it took on a European dimension. Links were established between Streets of Brighton and French festivals in Amiens, Sotteville-lès-Rouen and Béthune. This facilitated what Jean-Pierre Marcos, a French artistic director, describes as "a unique European project, The European Polycentre of Artistic Creation (PECA)." [24]

Although the Streets of Brighton is no longer running, in recent years, the Brighton Festival's emphasis on alternative culture and unusual platforms and spaces has continued to strengthen. Jane McMorrow highlights that:

❛What started as a highly reputable but fairly conventional arts festival has changed remarkably in the last few years into something more unexpected, more daring and, I think, more dangerous. That's the reason why the Festival has acquired the international reputation it has in recent years.

Though we've got a world-class performance space in the Brighton Dome, the Festival has also been pushing the boundaries not just of what art should be, but where it should be [...] It's now a given to say that Brighton Festival doesn't just happen indoors, in places where you expect art to be, it happens just about everywhere, on pavements, in squares, on the beach, on hillsides, on its estates, in the Marina ... It's extraordinary how quickly the Festival's ever-hungry audience has grown to expect ever more daring performances [...] it's about reimagining an ordinary place we all know well – adding a whole new experience to the city we live in [...] Brighton is no longer the place that just hosts the Festival. Brighton itself is now the stage. ' [25]

Brighton Fringe

' Brighton Festival has "grown so much [...] that now we do indeed look like a second Edinburgh – with the Fringe very much in its place and quite separately convened and organised." '
GAVIN HENDERSON[26]

Although alternative acts have been part of the Brighton Festival for a long time, the Festival Fringe was originally established as a marginal celebration of alternative culture. Fringe activity has been running alongside Brighton Festival since it began in 1967. Now, Brighton Fringe is the largest open-access arts festival in England, featuring all forms of art and performance by both new and emerging talent.

Brighton Fringe's "mission is to bring artists and audiences together and act as a catalyst for creativity."[27] As well as providing a platform for artists to showcase their work, Brighton Fringe supports artistic development through free workshops, mentoring schemes and bursary programmes.

In 2018, the Fringe consisted of 1,008 events in 164 venues across the city and attracted over 596,000 audience members.[28]

Otherplace and The Warren

Each year during Brighton Fringe, Otherplace, Brighton's largest production company, presents The Warren, a pop-up festival site and puts on shows in venues across the city. Staging 710 performances across four venues for Brighton Fringe 2018,[29] The Warren is now Brighton Fringe's biggest venue, with over 20% of the Fringe programme taking place at its venues and bars.[30]

Performance art: breaking down the boundaries between art and theatre

Although Brighton comes alive with alternative culture during the Festivals in May, alternative performance and theatre have long been taking place in the city throughout the year. Performance art was an important feature of Brighton's alternative cultural scene and a fundamental part of the Zap's programme all-year round.

The term "performance art" became widely used during the 1970s to describe an interdisciplinary form of creative expression which combines different creative mediums, such as live theatre, art, music and recording.

These live, multi-layered artistic experiences sometimes aim to convey a particular message, perhaps related to politics or ideology. Pieces can also take a more light-hearted form, sometimes serving as what Dennis De Groot, an original member of Ddart Performance Art, terms a "gesture": an expression of an idea or "a way of seeing the world" for pure entertainment with no underlying agenda or meaning. De Groot emphasises the form's egalitarian nature; performance art challenges established ideas of who can perform and where, with performances often taking part in unusual or everyday public spaces, rather than traditional theatres, galleries or specifically designated sites.[31]

The Brighton Combination: Brighton's Art Lab Space

One of the city's most iconic and well-known alternative theatre companies was the Brighton Combination. During the 1960s, radical playwright and director Noël Greig was "looking to find a context for theatre to happen that wasn't in a conventional performance space."[32] In 1968, Greig, along with two friends, Jenny Harris and Ruth Marks, established the first alternative theatre company with its own building and ensemble, the Brighton Combination. Upon acquiring an old Victorian school house and some outhouses at 76 West Street in Brighton for what Greig describes as "a peppercorn rent", they transformed the space "into an Arts Lab on nothing"[33] and established "a 'producing' fringe theatre."[34]

The alley where The Combination once stood, located to the right of the Family Leisure Arcade at 76 West Street. *Backstage Brighton*, 2010, QueenSpark Books.

Described as "Brighton's answer to Edinburgh's Traverse",[35] the Brighton Combination drew its inspiration from "the ambiance and ethos" of Jim Haynes's Art Lab in Drury Lane and the likes of the Little Theatre in St Martin's Lane.[36]

In an interview, Jenny Harris reflects on how the Brighton Combination's target audience shaped the work they produced:

> ❝ ... it was for a different demographic, different audience, younger people [...] You know, working class [...] kids. We were trying to completely deconstruct theatre and reconstruct it again in what we now remember as Studio Theatres and what we would now call "site specific" and what we would now call "outdoor festivals" and "street art" and "street shows" and getting people involved. Getting

 [37]

Reflecting the company's strong left-wing, alternative ethos, the plays which took to the Brighton Combination's stage were often radical. Alternative companies on tour performed there, including Portable Theatre, People Show, Incubus, Wherehouse La MaMa, Freehold and Inter-Action. One of the Brighton Combination's first productions was Michael Almaz's *The Rasputin Show*, which earned them national attention. The company also devised their own pieces, such as the meta, self-aware critique of contemporary theatre, *The Don't Come Show*.[38] Among the Brighton Combination's writers was Howard Brenton, whose work went on to be produced on a large scale both nationally and in Europe[39]:

> '... it was here that Howard Brenton and Richard Crane would cut their teeth, and here I sat on a rough wooden bench for a new play by Günter Grass and later realised that the man with the big bushy moustache, sitting next to me, was none other than the author.' GAVIN HENDERSON[40]

Alongside the main theatre and several other rooms with events from films and poetry readings to discos going on, the trio also managed a café to ensure financial security.[41] Greig recalls the dedication this required:

> '... you'd go in in the morning, early, you'd prepare all the food, you'd cook all the food, you'd go and rehearse, and then those people who weren't in the play would be serving the food in the evening, you'd do the play.' [42]

Greig also highlights the importance of the possibilities offered by the versatile space in West Street:

> '... we re-configured all the time, we didn't turn it into a conventional theatre, it was a black box, it was one of the first black boxes. It changed all the time, we did different things with it. Then we'd do the play and then move everything around and we'd show a film, we had an old projector and we'd show films, radical films, and then [...] we'd turn it into a dance space and have light shows. This would go on 'til three in the morning, we'd have a few joints, go to bed, get up the next day and do it all again!' [43]

The Brighton Combination's activities were not just contained to Brighton; they performed at a range of venues on tours, including the Arts Theatre, Drury Lane Arts Lab, universities, colleges and various Trade Union organisations. Touring broadened their audiences to include young people, students, national alternative theatre practitioners and Trade Unionists.[44]

In 1971, the company moved to The Albany in Deptford, south east London, dropping "Brighton" from their name to become the Combination, and continued their work there until 1990.

The 1980s: a difficult time for the arts

Gavin Henderson recalls that in the context of the "accountancy culture" which characterised the Thatcher era in the 1980s and its "chilly message for [...] the arts", "artists began to reappear in abundance", proving that "art is a mineral that forms under pressure."[45] Performance poet Roger Ely recalls

Neil Butler's excitement when "new work" began to emerge at this time. It was not only the "street/ outside/ site-specific nature" of the work which was so exciting, but also the fact that "artists chose to present their work in pubs and clubs and not exclusively in art galleries or traditional theatres." This "Art" challenged elitist and traditional forms of art by addressing "new audiences in a direct fashion."[46]

Pub performances at Grand Central Pub and The Marlborough

During the 1980s, the Nightingale Theatre and The Marlborough pub "gave the town's huge community of actors a basis of work experience."[47] The Nightingale Theatre was originally located above Grand Central Pub in Surrey Street:

> ‘In the mid-1980s a whole string of women's theatre groups came to perform there. For me the best was Siren Theatre Company, a Brighton-based lesbian theatre group, who started out putting on plays about the role of women in our society and graduated on to lesbian drama. It was very inspiring. ’ LINDA, LESBIAN ACTIVIST[48]

Although the Nightingale has since relocated from its pub setting, theatre continues to be performed at The Marlborough pub and theatre in Prince's Street. The building has a complex and fascinating history, dating back to 1794; it has served as a ballroom and gambling suite, as well as a meeting place for activists and artists. Since the 1960s, it has had close links with the LGBTQ+ community, which is reflected in its contemporary programme.[49]

The Marlborough Theatre sign, 2019 by Evlynn Sharp.

With a theatre programme as diverse and unusual as its history, The Marlborough showcases a range of work from cabaret, music and comedy to literary performances, featuring local talent and artists from further afield, in its upstairs 55-seat theatre. Since 2010, the theatre has been run by Community Interest Company, Marlborough Productions, who works with LGBTQ+ practitioners. The Marlborough's programme focuses on Live Art & Performance Art, especially pioneering work commenting on contemporary queer life.

The Marlborough was the base for the Pink Fringe production company, which ran events at Brighton Fringe until 2015. Its programme was curated "on an open-access basis", with the aim of "challeng[ing] perceptions around diverse work, specifically art created by and about queer & LGBT people, placing it in multiple contexts, some familiar, some new and unusual, with the aim of attracting new audiences."[50]

Cliffhanger Theatre Company: theatre "at the edge"

Cliffhanger Theatre Company also performed in rooms above pubs, as well as in the street. Emerging around the same time as Neil Butler's Contemporary Festival of Arts in the 1980s, Cliffhanger made "new shows for the small-scale touring circuit" and helped to establish "Brighton's shoreline" as a "metaphor" for theatrical work "at the edge."[51]

The Company's work often took the form of comic sketches or pastiches of popular genres such as 1950s science fiction films and television soap opera. Their show *Gymslip Vicar* proved popular at Edinburgh Fringe and was nominated for the 1984 Olivier Award for Best Comedy.

Being part of the Company provided valuable experience for its members' future careers in creative industries. Robin Driscoll went on to co-author *Mr Bean* and Pete McCarthy became a best-selling author and TV presenter,[52] having "cut his comic teeth in the vanguard of the alternative comedy boom of the Eighties" with Cliffhanger.[53]

Yes/No Productions and STOMP at the Old Market Theatre

Pete McCarthy introduced founding members of the percussion group, STOMP, Luke Cresswell and Steve McNicholas.[54] Having originally met during rehearsals at the Old Market Theatre in Hove, the duo now owns this venue, which provides a base for their international production company, Yes/No Productions. Founded in 1992, Yes/No Productions grew out of Yes/No People band and now works across entertainment media and platforms. It originally managed STOMP, a world-renowned rhythm-based show, which uniquely combines percussion, movement and visual comedy.

Cresswell and McNicholas saved the Grade II-listed building from being demolished or converted into flats

The Old Market Theatre, 2019 by Evlynn Sharp.

with the aim of keeping it as an arts venue.[55] Cresswell recalls their decision to purchase the theatre:

> ' We used this place for rehearsing many-a-time [...] We also recorded here a lot before we bought the place; the sound in the room is fantastic, so we recorded our film scores there, with strings [...] There was talk of it becoming anything but a venue, and we just thought that was wrong. We thought it would be nice to keep it running as a venue, and that was the reason to buy it, to keep it running as a venue and as a space we could keep using [...] Now it's a really nice 300-seater or 500 standing venue. ' [56]

Neon-lit frontage of the Komedia, 2010 by Roz South.

The Old Market is now one of Brighton and Hove's leading music and theatre venues, providing a flexible multi-purpose space with in-house video and audio recording facilities.

Komedia

"Brighton's post-Zap mainstream fringe venue"[57], Komedia, was also established during the 1990s and soon became internationally renowned. Since being founded in 1994, it has played a key role in establishing the comedy careers of many household names, including Graham Norton, Mel and Sue, Johnny Vegas, Al Murray, Michael McIntyre, Sarah Millican, Russell Howard, Armstrong and Miller, Jenny Éclair, Alistair McGowan and Omid Djalili.

Inspired by their experiences of European Café Theatre venues, Colin Granger, Marina Kobler and David Lavender, who was involved with the Nightingale during the 1980s, converted a Grade II-listed Georgian billiard hall in Kemp Town into a theatre and cabaret bar. Rapidly gaining popularity, Komedia moved to a larger space in the former Tesco supermarket in Gardner Street in 1998. This enabled the development of its programme of live entertainment, music, comedy, cabaret and theatre shows, as well as attracting big names such as Arctic Monkeys, the Mighty Boosh, Steven Berkoff, Julian Cope and Harry Hill.

As its national reputation grew, Komedia became involved in Edinburgh Festival Fringe. When in 2000, Richard Daws, formerly of Victoria Real television production company, joined, Komedia Entertainment was founded to manage and produce new comedy acts. Komedia has since opened a second European Café Theatre style venue in Bath and formed a creative partnership with Picturehouse. This partnership has seen the art house cinema group opening Duke's at Komedia, a two-screen state of the art cinema within Komedia Brighton and a screen in Komedia Bath.[58]

Brighton Little Theatre

As well as larger-scale production companies, Brighton has also long been home to small companies producing shows in venues across the city, some of whom are still performing today. One of these is Brighton Little Theatre.

Technical glitches can cause problems for any theatre company. But what about power cuts threatening to plunge productions into darkness without warning? Or war-time call-ups meaning that cast members could be lost at any moment? These were exactly the challenges faced by not-for-profit company Brighton Little Theatre, which has produced continuously since 1940, withstanding the challenges of war-time and post-war austerity.

This shared determination, as well as a passion for theatre, brought a group of young people together in 1940 to produce and perform plays. The group initially met in a basement flat in Denmark Terrace in Brighton but were later able to rent the Studio Theatre in Clarence Gardens, which has been home to the Brighton Little Theatre ever since. Because of its association with artists and painting, the theatre was originally called Brighton Little Studio Theatre. In the 1980s, the current name was adopted.

Over the years, the company has tended to perform an average of eight or nine plays per year, ranging from classic to contemporary. New facilities have created additional opportunities for the theatre to thrive, expanding its activities to include youth theatre groups, play readings, workshops and social events.

From candle-lit performances and soundtracks hummed by stage-crews in the place of a radio during the era of post-war austerity, being part of Brighton Little Theatre has created many memories for its members.[59]

Performer Philip Burnard recalls his experience of another company who shared the same name:

> ‘In 1965, me and a group of friends found ourselves invited to join the Brighton Little Theatre, not to be confused with the theatre company in Clarence Gardens established in 1940. It was organised and run by two

Brighton Little Theatre, 2019 by Daren Kay.

New Venture Theatre, 2019 by Evlynn Sharp.

New Venture Theatre

The New Venture Theatre in Bedford Place, near Hove, was originally a church school. When the church was destroyed by fire, the company took on the rent of the first floor of the old school and it became the company's permanent home in 1958, with productions continuing in the main theatre on the first floor. When, in 1981, the church decided to sell the building, money was raised enabling New Venture Theatre to purchase it. Today, performances take place in the Ground Floor Theatre and the Upstairs Theatre, which reopened in 2013, with all major productions open to the public. As well as staging around 10 productions each season, New Venture Theatre also holds a number of social events during the year as well as workshops, play readings and a weekly acting class:[61]

Brighton Open Air Theatre (BOAT): taking theatre outside

Brighton Open Air Theatre is the city's only open-air theatre. The 425-seat venue represents the realisation of the long-held ambition of Brighton playwright and construction manager, Adrian Bunting, who tragically died of pancreatic cancer in May 2013, aged 47. Following his diagnosis, Adrian dedicated himself to designing a venue and identifying the ideal site, selecting an abandoned bowling green in Dyke Road Park. He left his life savings to four friends – Steve Turner, Claire Raftery, James Payne and Donna Close – to see his dream through.[63] His friends raised a further £100,000 and saw the project through to completion. BOAT was opened by Adrian's mother, Isobelle Bunting, in May 2015.[64]

Remaining true to Bunting's vision of an open artistic policy, BOAT showcases a mix of productions from amateur to Shakespeare's Globe, to circus and music. Since its opening, over 25,000 people have visited the theatre and it is now well-established as part of Brighton and Hove's cultural landscape, with performances from both local and international companies.

Dreamthinkspeak: performance in spaces beyond the theatre

If any Brighton-based theatre company embodies and epitomises the idea of using alternative spaces for performance, it is dreamthinkspeak. The internationally acclaimed company has been a pioneer in "site-responsive" theatre across the world since forming in 1999, putting on performances in the former Co-Op store (now Poundland) on London Road, an underground abattoir in Clerkenwell, a disused paper factory and the Old Treasury Building in Perth, Australia. Producing the work of its artistic director, Tristan Sharps, performances are large-scale and artistically ambitious, combining live performance, film and installations to create remarkable and memorable experiences for audiences.[65] Using the specificity of the space and its architecture, performances take audiences on a physical and conceptual journey and invite them to reconsider and re-engage with familiar or forgotten spaces in new ways.

Fairground at night with Star Wheel, The Level, 1993. QueenSpark Books.

Notes

1 J.M. Woodham, N. Butler, R. Ely, L. Aggiss, I. Smith, S. Fanshawe, S. Thomas, et al., *ZAP: Twenty-Five Years of Innovation*, (Brighton: QueenSpark Books, 2007).

2 Jonathan M. Woodham, 'The "Art College" Basement: some recollections', *University of Brighton*.

3 Ibid.

4 *ZAP: Twenty-Five Years of Innovation*.

5 Ibid.

6 Ibid.

7 'What's On: Festival '79 Brighton July-21-28', *Brighton Voice*, July 1979, QueenSpark Archives.

8 *ZAP: Twenty-Five Years of Innovation*.

9 Jo Wadsworth, 'Brighton Festival: 50 years of "a city on the edge"', *The Telegraph*, 25 February 2016.

10 Andrew Comben, 'Brighton Festival: 50 years of "a city on the edge"'.

11 Ibid.

12 Gerry Holloway and Frank Jackson, *Open House: A historical survey of the Fiveways Artists Group*, (Brighton: More Than Ninety Minutes Publishing, 1999), p. 40.

13 'Brighton Festival: 50 years of "a city on the edge"'.

14 *Open House*, p. 41.

15 *ZAP: Twenty-Five Years of Innovation*.

16 Ibid.

17 Ibid.

18 Ibid.

19 Ibid.

20 Ibid.

21 Ibid.

22 Ibid.

23 Ibid.

24 Ibid.

25 Ibid.

26 Brighton Fringe, 'Brighton Fringe Info'.

27 Ibid.

28 Ibid.

29 Otherplace, 'About'.

30 Brighton Fringe, 'The Warren'.

31 'The Fine Art of Performance: Living Legacies of UK Art Schools' event, produced by Prof. Gavin Butt, Attenborough Centre for the Creative Arts, University of Sussex, 20/02/2019.

32 Unfinished Histories, 'Brighton Combination'.

33 Ibid.

34 *ZAP: Twenty-Five Years of Innovation*.

35 Ibid.

36 Noël Greig, 'Brighton Combination', *Unfinished Histories*.

37 Tony Coult: interview with Jenny Harris, 'Brighton Combination', *Unfinished Histories*.

38 Noel Greig, 'Brighton Combination', *Unfinished Histories*.

39 Howard Barker, 'Grey Theatre', *Brighton Voice*, no. 6, 1973, QueenSpark Archives.

40 *ZAP: Twenty-Five Years of Innovation*.

41 'Brighton Combination', *Unfinished Histories*.

42 Ibid.

43 Ibid.

44 Ibid.

45 *ZAP: Twenty-Five Years of Innovation*.

46 Ibid.

47 Ibid.

48 My Brighton and Hove, 'Memories of the Siren Theatre Company.'

49 The Marlborough Pub and Theatre, 'About Us'.

50 The Marlborough Pub and Theatre, 'Pink Fringe'.

51 Gavin Henderson, *ZAP: Twenty-Five Years of Innovation*.

52 Ibid.

53 The Argus, 'Pete McCarthy and the alternative comedy boom of the Eighties: Goodbye to a genius', *The Argus*, 9 October 2004.

54 Ibid.

55 Yes/No Productions, 'Yes/No: What we do'.

56 Jeff Hemmings, 'Stomp – Interview 2015', *Brighton's Finest*.

57 Gavin Henderson, *ZAP: Twenty-Five Years of Innovation*.

58 Komedia, 'History'.

59 Brighton Little Theatre, 'Who We Are'.

60 Philip Burnard, 'Brighton Little Theatre', *My Brighton and Hove*.

61 The New Venture Theatre, 'About Us'.

62 *Latest Brighton*, 'Stage: Brighton's New Venture Theatre is never shy of tackling classic theatre'.

63 Brighton Open Air Theatre, 'History of BOAT'.

64 Andrew Stuckey, 'Q&A with Anne-Marie Williams, Manager at Brighton Open Air Theatre', *Ticket Source*.

65 dreamthinkspeak, 'About'.

GARDNER STREET
Infinity Foods
Workers Co-operative
Infinity Foods
ty Foods
ty Foods
SHOP
Infinity Foods
PEDESTRIAN
ZONE
Sat 10am - 7pm
Sun & Bank
Holidays
11am - 5pm
SEEDY
SUNDAY
Closed
INNOVATORS

Infinity Foods, c.2019 by Kavitha Ravikumar.

chapter 6
Gill Ditch

 in the latter half of the 18th century. When looking back at the history of the city it is interesting to note the variety of people who were attracted to the town, and what encouraged them to stay and make a life in Brighton. As an early destination for those interested in their well-being, Brighton was championed by Dr Richard Russell. He was interested in the benefits of drinking seawater and bathing in it and even published a book on the subject.

Dr Richard Russell

Dr Richard Russell's book that promoted the benefits of sea bathing was published in the 18th century:

> Russell was the foremost proponent of the 'sea water cure' which brought Brighton to prominence in the 1750s. This doctor was instrumental in reviving the fortunes of the poor fishing town of Brighton in the mid-eighteenth century. [1]

Russell suggested to his patients that they visit Brighton to participate in the sea water cure. His reputation grew and the numbers increased to such an extent that in 1753 Russell felt it was worthwhile setting up in a house in the Steine facing the sea, currently the site of the Royal Albion Hotel.

Another key influence on visitors coming to Brighton was the Prince Regent, who went on to become George IV. He began to visit Brighton frequently in the late 18th century and

Dr Richard Russell by Benjamin Wilson, c.1755. Royal Pavilion & Museums.

his increasing fondness for the town prompted the upgrade of his residence, the Marine Pavilion, to the opulent and idiosyncratic Royal Pavilion, using the prevailing trend for Chinoiserie decoration. Wherever the Prince went so did his court, and as the more affluent crowd began to visit so more attractions and accommodation were needed. Hotels had to expand and adapt in order to cope with those who were drawn to the bathing and the races, and visitors who stayed for the season often required more permanent places to stay. Local entrepreneurs accommodated their needs with the completion of the Kemptown and Brunswick terraces.

Sake Deen Mahomed

The arrival of the railway in 1841 added to the numbers of visitors arriving in the town. One such individual was Sake Deen Mahomed who opened Vapour Baths on the site where the Queen's Hotel, Kings Road currently stands. At that time even the more sophisticated homes did not generally contain rooms especially for washing; as a consequence, the more affluent visitors to Brighton were introduced to the practice of shampooing via the Vapour Baths. The baths were also promoted as helping to relieve a number of conditions:

> The Indian Medicated Vapour Bath, according to Mahomed, was "a cure to many diseases and giving full relief when everything fails; particularly rheumatic and paralytic, gout, stiff joints, old sprains, lame legs, aches and pains in the joints." [2]

The Vapour Baths became very successful and Sake Deen Mahomed was appointed as a shampooing surgeon to George IV. George was so convinced by the

Sake Deen Mahomed by Thomas Mann Baynes, c.1810. Royal Pavilion & Museums.

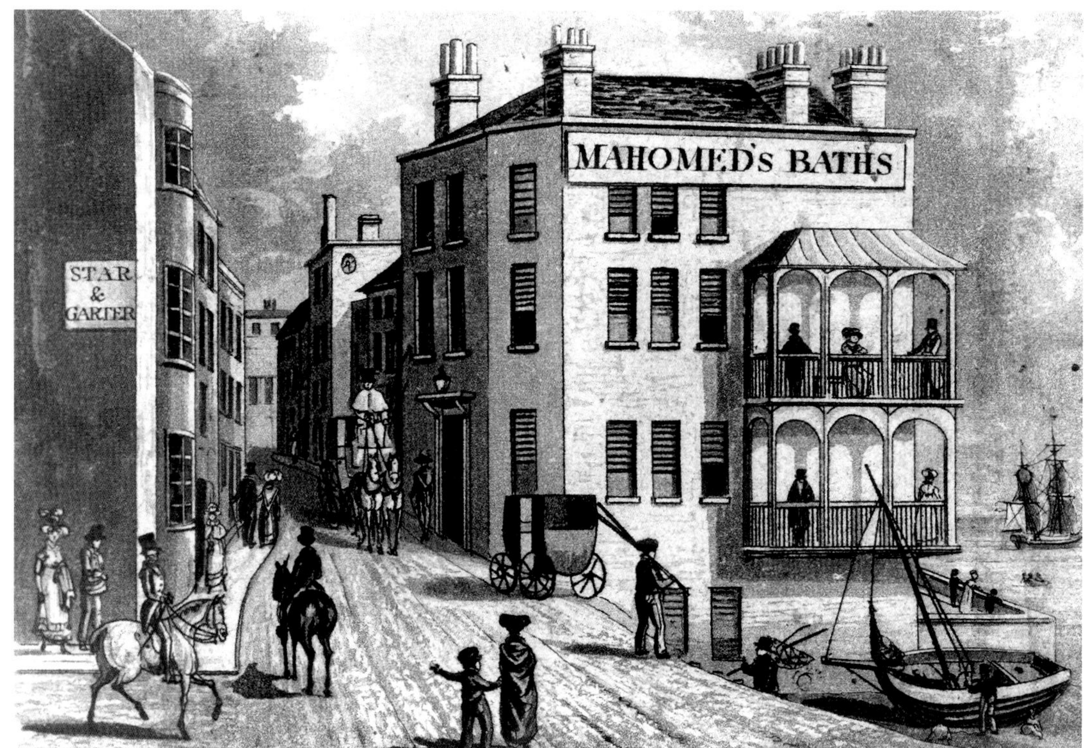

Sake Deen Mahomed's Baths, Brighton, early 19th Century. Royal Pavilion & Museums.

benefits of bathing that he installed vapour and sea water baths in the Royal Pavilion:

> ‘Having patronage from the King assisted Sake Deen Mahomed in gaining a reputation in Brighton and, attracting an important *clientèle* that ensured prosperity not only for himself, but for others involved in the bathing industry.’ [3]

Magnus Volk

The arrival of the railway led to a wider range of people discovering the joys of the seaside and Brighton; it also attracted the inventor Magnus Volk, who moved to the town. He became renowned for his interest in technology and was responsible for introducing new inventions:

> ‘An eccentric inventor, Volk was a pioneer of the early of use electricity. He brought the first telephone service to Brighton in 1879 and fitted his home in Preston Road with electricity in 1880. In 1883 Volk opened his famous seafront railway which was a terrific success. Perhaps his most remarkable invention was the so called, ‘Daddy Longlegs’. This was a railway that ran

Magnus Volk, at 85 years old, 1937. Royal Pavilion and Museums.

with its rails in the sea between Brighton and Rottingdean. It was the world's first publicly operated electric railway when it opened and was quite a revolutionary idea.' [4]

Volk's railway still runs today and transports many seaside visitors between the Aquarium and Black Rock.

Phoebe Hessel

Brighton became home for one woman who dared to be different; Phoebe Hessel spent time living in Brighton in the 18th century and is buried in St Nicholas' churchyard, Brighton. She did not follow the pathway generally expected of women born in that era:

'Phoebe Hessel was born in Stepney, East London in March 1713. At that time the world was very different from how it is today. Women and men were expected to lead very different lives. Phoebe Hessel was a woman who spent part of her life dressed as a man. There are two different reasons given for why she did this. Her father taught her to play the fife and drum and, as she grew up Phoebe became a soldier. She fought in many battles dressed as a man.' [5]

'After many years she was badly injured in her arm at the battle of Fontenoy in Belgium in 1745. Later

Etching of Phoebe Hessel, c.1814. Royal Pavilion & Museums.

that year she left the army. She went to live in
Plymouth where she married Samuel Goldin and
had nine children. After Samuel died she went to
live in Brighton where she married Thomas Hessel,
who made a living by fishing. When Thomas
died, Phoebe bought a donkey and sold fish and
vegetables in the villages around Brighton to make
enough money to live on. When she got very
old she sold toys, oranges and gingerbread near
Brighton Pavilion to make money. Because she was
so famous, Prince George, the Prince Regent, gave
her a pension of ½ a Guinea a week when she was
95 years old in 1808.' [6]

The Body Shop Founder Anita Roddick. From the Roddick Foundation.

Anita Roddick

Another innovative woman who dared to be different
and made her mark on the city was Anita Roddick
who started The Body Shop chain in Brighton. Anita
was interested in shampoos and cosmetics made of
natural materials that did not irritate the skin or harm
the environment. In 1976, she started to create her
own products, sold in plastic containers that could
be easily refilled, from a small shop in Kensington
Gardens, Brighton. From this tiny space in one of the
town's oldest shopping areas, Roddick went on to
create a global chain of stores:

'The very first The Body Shop store was opened
by Anita Roddick on the 27th March 1976 at
22 Kensington Gardens. At the beginning it
only sold a range of 25 different products with
an emphasis on natural ingredients that were
ethically sourced and cruelty free. Customers
were encouraged to take the plastic bottles which
contained their potions back to be re-filled.
Roddick promoted this practice as recycling;
in truth she started it because she did not have
enough plastic bottles.' [7]

> 'I remember using the Body Shop when
> it first opened in 1976; using natural
> products and being able to re-fill bottles
> was a great idea and fitted in with my
> ideals. I remember meeting Anita and
> talking to her in the shop about the
> different oils used and their benefits.'
> GILL DITCH

Infinity Foods

Many visitors who come to Brighton for the day are attracted to the wide range of food establishments, but back in the 1970s there were not that many options for vegetarians outside major cities. Fortunately, that was about to change. Infinity Foods became the place to go for vegetarians and many others to buy food supplies:

'Back in 1970, two friends – Ian Loeffler and Peter Deadman opened a macrobiotic café at the University of Sussex called *Biting Through*, which led to a demand for the ingredients they were using in their cooking. The following year, Peter, along with Jenny Deadman & Robin Bines opened a small shop called Infinity Foods in a converted terraced house in Church Street, Brighton. Here they sold basic vegetarian whole foods and freshly baked products. The business grew and grew and by 1973, the business needed to expand and it moved to its current site in North Road. The store gained a wider reputation when it moved sites as more people became aware of the foods it sold and the ideals used to keep it running.' [8]

'Infinity Foods was considered the alternative place food venue of Brighton, stocking grains,

Workers at Infinity Foods, c.1976 by Peter Deadman.

beans, and things hard or impossible to obtain elsewhere. It also sold delicious home-made peanut butter and a limited supply of organically-grown vegetables **9** [9]

> **'As a young student in the 1970s Infinity Foods was the face of healthy eating. They made the best wholemeal bread and muesli which helped keep you going when you had a small budget. I am still a customer and as soon as I walk in there I am transported back in time by the smell of the bread. It typifies the spirit of Brighton to me as it dared to do something different and is still run on the original co-operative principles.'** GILL DITCH

Brighton Voice in July 1976 commented on the rising popularity of Infinity Foods:

> Infinity Foods, the Whole Food Shop in Brighton, has become extremely popular of late, they started about 5 years ago in a very small way. Now with the great rise in popularity of whole foods Infinity foods are so busy that you can hardly move in the shop on a Saturday. **9** [10]

HISBE

In the 21st century, Brighton people are still innovating in the way of shopping and buying food. HISBE, which stands for How It Should Be, was set up by two Brighton sisters Amy and Ruth Anslow, in 2013. The HISBE website explains their mission and why they are not like other supermarkets:

> We're not a health food shop. We're not an exclusively vegan or vegetarian food shop. We're a regular supermarket – operating how it should be. And we want to transform the food industry by challenging the way big supermarkets do business. We won't bombard you with hundreds of products all owned by a handful of giant corporations. Call us rebellious, but how many versions of the same cornflake, porridge oat, loo roll and baked bean do we need?

HISBE, 2019 by Kavitha Ravikumar.

We're a social enterprise. A Community Interest Company (CIC) doing business for good. Business beyond profits we call it. We make a positive contribution to the local food system and the local economy. We're all about making good food more accessible and affordable. We champion a fair and sustainable food industry, and we put customers, suppliers, and staff first. ' [11]

' Amy and Ruth have benefitted from mentoring from the Body Shop's co-founder, Gordon Roddick. He approached the sisters after hearing about HISBE. With a background in ethical trading, Gordon has provided the sisters with invaluable advice which has enabled them to take their social enterprise from strength to strength. ' [12]

Big Lemon Bus Company

The Big Lemon is a Community Interest Company, established in 2006, which provides environmentally-sustainable bus services in Brighton and Hove. It operates six local bus routes in the city as well as local and national coach services, walking trips and holidays.

Originally the buses ran on waste cooking oil, recycled from local restaurants, but in 2017 The Big Lemon launched the UK's first solar-powered electric bus. The company's entire bus fleet is slowly being converted to electricity, generated from solar panels on the roof of the bus depot. [13]

Big Lemon Bus and the Company's founder Tom Druitt.

'I first came across The Big Lemon Bus company when they had recently started up. They came along to a school careers event I had organised with their bus fuelled by used chip oil. The teenagers loved the idea and were fascinated as to how it was set up by Tom Druitt; he was a real inspiration to them.' GILL DITCH

UnLtd The Bevy lunch club & music, 2019 by Nina Emett/FotoAgency.

The Bevy in Brighton

Spaces for people to meet up and support each other are still being created all over the city. In recent years The Bevy is one such place that has been created and supported by the community:

> ❛Re-opened by the community in 2014 after being shut by the police, The Bevy is the only community owned pub on a housing estate in the UK.
>
> Funded by hundreds of community shareholders and refurbished by volunteers, it's so much more than a boozer. In one typical week, The Bevy delivered meals to older residents kept at home by snow, ran family cooking lessons, hosted lunch clubs, an arts and craft session, a parkrun, a local MPs surgery, smoking-cessation clinics, and a free bus service to the local football club, Brighton & Hove Albion. As well as serving food and beers, it's home to darts and bar billiards teams.

Operating as a social hub for the 18,000 residents of Moulsecoomb and Bevendean, The Bevy is a blueprint of how pubs can turn the tide of closures.

We had visitors from London looking at setting up a community pub. Our customers put up hanging baskets, fixed broken doors and lights because it is their pub. ❜ WARREN, THE BEVY[14]

Free University Brighton

A reduction in courses offered by Higher and Further Education coupled with rising tuition fees has led to a series of community initiatives experimenting in free, alternative education:

Free University Brighton students and tutors, 2015 by Ali Ghanimi.

> Free University Brighton (FUB) was founded in 2012 as a practical response to the trebling of university fees and cuts to adult education. A cooperative run by volunteers, FUB provides an alternative system of free education, up to degree-level. FUB's aim is to provide democratic, accessible and socially useful education by turning public spaces into classrooms, enabling communities to come together to think, develop, learn, enquire, question the world around them and to explore how it could be different and better. ALI GHANIMI, FUB[15]

Coachwerks

Brighton is a city that has championed the development of artists and performers through the creation of events such the Brighton Festival, Fringe Festival, The Zap and the Artists' Open Houses. It also champions the use of spaces for development of such talent. Coachwerks is one such space:

> Coachwerks began as an arts and workshop space in 2008 and over the years, it has been home to dozens of artists and crafts-people. The building has been through an almost endless cycle of change, at one time housing a cooperative brewery and bar, a vegan café and a venue for musicians, film-makers and other community events. At the time of writing it is a gallery for artists, a space for workshops and houses a whole-food shop run by volunteers. [16]

Brighton in the 21st century is a place that works to support and incubate innovators who are developing businesses that follow ethical principles and support different groups within the community.

Coachwerks in Hollingdean, 2019
by Ali Ghanimi.

Notes

1 Carder, Tim. 1990. "Dr Richard Russell." https://www.mybrightonandhove.org.uk.

2 Drury, J. 2012. "Sake Deen Mahomed." https://www.mybrightonandhove.org.uk.

3 Ibid.

4 Drury, J. 2006. "Magnus Volk, Famous Inventor." https://www.mybrightonandhove.org.uk.

5 Moorhouse, Ruth, and Chris Randall. 1994. *Her Story: The Life of Phoebe Hessel.* Brighton: QueenSpark Books.

6 Ibid.

7 Drury, J. 2012. "Do you remember the shop?" https://www.mybrightonandhove.org.uk.

8 Foods, Infinity. 2016. "Infinity Foods Story." Infinity Foods Retail.

9 Noyce, John, and Francis Jarman. 1973. *Alternative Brighton.* Radical Brighton.

10 *Brighton Voice*, July 76.

11 Anslow, Amy, and Ruth Anslow. 2019. *HISBE.*

12 Loans, Start up. 2013. *Food and Drink Retail .*

13 The Big Lemon, https://thebiglemon.com.

14 Warren, The Bevy, April 2019. https://www.thebevy.co.uk.

15 Ali Ghanimi, Free University Brighton. https://freeuniversitybrighton.org/about.

16 https://coachwerks.org/coachwerkers.

Photo of the blue plaque honouring Anita Roddick at 22 Kensington Gardens, 2019 by Kavitha Ravikumar.

VISUAL
CULTURE

Brighton street, 2019 by Evlynn Sharp.

chapter 7

Siobhán Laroche

 being an "arty" place and a hub of creativity. The city's brightly coloured buildings and street murals give a clue to its wealth of creative talent and innovation. What is unique about Brighton are the spaces where artistic creation takes place, enabling the city's population to engage with the arts in a myriad of ways, not simply limited to visiting a gallery or exhibition.

Street Art

'The creativity of the city can't be confined within gallery walls' [1]

During the mid-1980s, Brighton was establishing itself as a key location on the UK street art scene as the phenomenon began to take off in urban areas across the country. From large murals covering the whole side of a building to more subtle motifs tucked away in alleyways, and telephone junction boxes decorated by Cassette Lord, people are bound to encounter street art in some form or another on a short walk through the city.

Amongst the work adorning the walls and spaces of the city are those by Banksy, Waleska and Vanessa Longchamp. The work of key Brighton street artists, including SNUB, Minty and REQ, can be seen across the city. Early graffiti was often found on railway lines and streets. Some murals have been commissioned but there are lots of spontaneous "throw ups", which are like tags, but often in more elaborate or bubble letters. The Brighton street art scene still retains links with that of the nearby capital, with some artists working in both cities, but for the most part, it has a freer, less controlled feel.

Other key locations for graffiti artists include The Level skate-park, which has been a hub of artistic activity since the 1980s.[2] Street art even goes beyond the streets to the seafront at Black Rock, where hoardings and a waste ground provide artists with a canvas.

In spite of the local council's clampdown on tagging during the 1990s, tags and throw ups are still seen frequently today. The authorities have provided some semi-legal locations for artists, too, including the sponsored mural on Kensington Street.

Veronica Stephens, Producer of Zap Art emphasises:

> ‘The power of street arts is great – it is accessible, inclusive and a great democratiser. It also has an amazing transformational quality and reinvigorates the places where people experience their day-to-day lives. Familiar sites take on a magical quality and become full of surprises.’ [3]

Within minutes of arriving in the city, visitors can hardly miss the rainbow coloured Prince Albert Pub on Trafalgar Street as they walk down from the station. The side wall of the pub is adorned with REQ's mural entitled *Icons* – a giant tribute to some of the biggest names in music. It is also the original location of Banksy's infamous *Kissing Policemen*, which is currently displayed in replica form, since the original was sold in 2014.

The narrow streets between Queen's Road and London Road are some of the best places to see street art; Gloucester Road, Kensington Street, Orange Row, Regent Street and North Road feature numerous wall murals. The courtyard spaces of 1960s office blocks in the area between London Road and New England Street also have their own fair share of street art.

RareKind

> ‘... perhaps the public face of graffiti in the UK for a lot of folk’ FED[4]

RareKind was a "collective of Brighton and London-based artists interested in graffiti and hip-hop orientated urban art."

"Independent artists in their own right", RareKind also played an important role in representing street art in the public domain and building the future of the street art scene. Their gallery in North Laine displayed "freehand-painted canvases, screen-printed and hand-printed clothing", while their shop stocked a "wide range of US and UK hip-hop on vinyl and CD, as well as books, magazines and DVDs."

RareKind also held monthly open mic/ deck nights and ran the "CanControl" scheme, partnering with local councils, schools and youth workers across the South East to organise graffiti art sessions for young people.[5]

Same Sky and Burning the Clocks

Bringing creativity and artistic creation to the streets of Brighton and into community spaces is also a key part of the work of Same Sky. Best known for producing the Children's Parade in May and the Burning the Clocks Parade in December, the award-winning community arts charity has been running since 1987 and is the largest of its kind in the South East. Working with schools, community groups, local authorities, arts festivals, businesses and individuals, they create large- and small-scale projects ranging from choreography and theatre to street parades, light shows and sculpture trails. Focusing on shared experiences, bringing people together through art and inspiring people's imaginations, Same Sky also equips people with practical skills to create their own art and artistic events. They often work with isolated members of communities, as well as those who have no history of involvement with art.[6]

Burning the Clocks, 2012
by Barry Pitman.

Burning the Clocks is a unique community event, which has taken place every year on 21st December since 1993, the shortest day of the year. It draws on pagan and anti-capitalist traditions to celebrate the festive season and the winter solstice. The city comes together to parade lanterns made of paper and willow, sold as kits by Same Sky, through the streets, accompanied by music and samba bands, before burning them on a huge bonfire on the seafront. Around 2,000 people take part in the parade and over 20,000 come to see the spectacle.[7] With its literal and symbolic associations of light in the dark of midwinter and bidding farewell to the previous year, this event is one of reflection as well as celebration.[8]

Artists' Open Houses Festival

While Brighton's public spaces provide canvases for street art and large-scale artistic events, the Artists' Open Houses festival in May sees artists' homes transformed into spaces where the public can engage with art:

Take a walk in a leafy suburb of Brighton, near the Fiveways junction on Ditchling Road, just north of the town centre, any weekend during the Brighton Festival in May and you will notice something unusual. These quiet Victorian and Edwardian streets, some modest, others more grand, are peppered with groups of people poring over maps. Others are walking up the garden paths of strangers' houses – houses which have banners proclaiming in a very un-English way that this house is open to the public. ❜ [9]

The Open Houses Festival is an annual event in which artists open up their homes to the public to showcase their artwork and discuss their methods and practices with visitors. Originating in the Fiveways area in 1982, it is now a city-wide phenomenon, granting the public access to art and the opportunity to engage in discussions with the artists who created it.

The festival's spirit is of openness and accessibility: "there are the usual students and connoisseurs but there are also people of all ages and backgrounds from the local community, many of them people who would not normally visit an art gallery."[10]

The variety of the work showcased matches the diversity of the visitors, ranging from paintings, sculpture, textiles, ceramics, jewellery and glass, among other artistic media. Unlike a gallery or museum, visitors do not just remain visitors; they can discuss the work with its creator, ask questions and even purchase it and take it home with them.[11] Artists themselves have also emphasised the value of these opportunities to discuss their work with the public in what can otherwise be a very solitary career.[12]

Inspired by artists who opened their studios to the public, which had been taking place since the 1960s,[13] Ned Hoskins began opening his house in Hollingbury Road to the public in 1982. Part of the inspiration behind this phenomenon was the city's lack of facilities for contemporary art exhibitions. Open studios had really taken off during Brighton Fringe in 1981, forming part of wider efforts by fringe groups within the Festival to make the art showcased more representative and relevant to local people.[14]

Hoskins's Open House gained significant interest from the city's residents and the local media.[15] Some of the artists who exhibited with Hoskins during the first year went on to open their own houses or join the Fiveways Artists Group, of which Hoskins was a member, in the years that followed.[16] The idea proved very popular with the visiting public and other trails connecting artists' houses soon sprang up around the city, and the Open Houses were born.

Other groups include Kemp Town, On the Level and Seven Dials, with which the Fiveways Group have co-operated.[17] Individual houses have also opened across the city. As the movement grew, Artists' Open Houses (AOH) was set up in 2004 by a small group of Open House artists, in order to produce a brochure detailing all the individual trails; their work now includes running a website, marketing and PR.

When Hoskins first opened his house, he noticed that "although there was great curiosity about what he was doing, people were reluctant to enter his private space."[18] Despite visitors' initial reservations, they soon realised that "artists lived in houses similar to their own and in ways similar to themselves."[19] It is this domestic setting which is key to both the concept and appeal of the Open Houses, providing a less intimidating and more accessible way of engaging with art.

Artist's Open House, 2018
by Idil Bozkurt.

As highlighted by the partner of a member of the Fiveways Artists Group, this initiative "blurs the divide between the public and the private." Artists have emphasised that it is important to retain the domestic quality of the exhibition space, rather than seeking to make it resemble a gallery by removing all of the furniture, for example. This sentiment is echoed by visitors; one remarked that it is valuable to "see how the art looks on an ordinary living room wall", making them "more likely to buy something at an Open House."[20]

In its use of an alternative artistic spaces, Open Houses plays a role in breaking down the idea of art as something refined and inaccessible, made by and for an élite. At an Open House, visitors are able to directly engage with the work and the person who made it and understand their creative processes. In this way, Open Houses play a role in "the movement to democratise the [Brighton] Festival", while also having a broader significance in putting "art and artists back on the map of daily life." Underlying the Open Houses' movement is a "commitment to making art accessible to as many people as possible and to enabling artists to exhibit their work to new audiences."[21]

Today, Artists' Open Houses takes place twice a year, during the Brighton Festival in May and in the run up to Christmas in December. Most of the houses belong to one of fourteen trails, which are grouped geographically, with venues within walking distance of each other.[22] There are now over 1,000 artists exhibiting in 200 venues across the city, as far as

Rottingdean, Newhaven, Ditchling, and beyond, making it virtually a festival in its own right. Similar Open Houses Festivals have also taken off in other cities across the UK.

Studio Collectives

During the 1980s, alongside the open houses and studios in Five Ways, "a host of studio collectives, with their own gallery spaces [...] emerged: North Star, Red Herring, Maze, and eventually Phoenix."[23] These spaces were crucial in enabling artists to create and exhibit their work and become part of artistic communities.

North Star Studio

The North Star Studio is Brighton's longest-running printmaking co-operative. The collective of printmakers and photographers have access to the Ditchling Road studio's presses and processing facilities. As a co-operative, members attend meetings, involving them in managing the space's upkeep and development, and making it a "friendly, fair and considerate democratic system." The studio also opens to the public as part of Brighton Fringe.[24]

Phoenix

Even though Brighton and Hove has one of the largest per-capita concentrations of creative businesses and professionals, high rent prices mean that affordable studio space is often hard to find. Organisations like Phoenix, which provide low-cost studio spaces for artists, are crucially important to the city's artistic community.

Founded by a group of artists in 1991, Phoenix is now the largest artist-led arts organisation in the South East.[25] The group initially rented around 20 workspaces in

Phoenix Brighton, 2018 by Kavitha Ravikumar.

Wellesley House, where they are still based today. After becoming a registered charity and company limited by guarantee in 1995, and with local council support and a Single Regeneration Budget grant, Phoenix purchased the building as a freehold. They then carried out significant refurbishment in order to create 100 studio workshop spaces for individual artists, gallery exhibition facilities and education workshop spaces. Alongside these spaces, there are now also larger workspaces for short-term projects. Phoenix's gallery and education programme brings the public into dialogue with artists and their work, featuring exhibitions of Phoenix artists' work, talks, family-friendly art markets and screenings of avant-garde art films.[26]

In December 1999, Red Herring and Maze studio groups began leasing a part of the building, whilst retaining their own identities and administration. Red Herring and Maze members have since become Phoenix members.[27]

Red Herring Studios

Also operating as a co-operative are Red Herring Studios, now based in Portslade. Managed, maintained and funded by its members for over 30 years, the co-operative has empowered over 200 artists to create and showcase their work by providing studio space and membership of an artistic community.

They first set up studios in the old Paragon photographic laboratory in West Street Brighton, in April 1985, with a vision of "providing working space and a community of interest for artists."[28]

The original seven members – Lucy Byatt, Jane Fordham, Jonathan Gilhooly, Christopher McHugh, Jon Mills, David Parfitt and Jane Pitt – and the new members who subsequently joined, worked hard to turn the old building into 23 individual studio spaces and a gallery on a very small budget. Initial self-curated and self-funded exhibitions included early solo shows by member Bruce Williams, Matthew Miller of Bear Road/Aleph Studios and Steve Geliot of Cross Street craft studios.

In 1986, the collective's second year, they curated two major projects for the Brighton Festival. These included *On All Fours*, a series of temporary installations by members in the old Bennett's hardware store in the North Laine, and *Brighton Studios '86* in Red Herring Gallery, a survey exhibition of all the artists' studios in Brighton, showcasing artwork and documenting the spaces' facilities, histories and members. This exhibition drew attention to the vibrancy and variety of artistic creation taking place across the city and brought about collaborations with other artists and organisations such as Bright Red Theatre Company, Carousel, Zap, and Open Studios, which in turn led to the creation of the Brighton Arts Forum.

Red Herring has since undertaken a rich and varied programme of group, solo and project exhibitions in various locations across the city. Current artists and makers include painters, sculptors, ceramicists and illustrators who have worked and showcased nationally and internationally as well as locally. Former members of the collective include artist Vong Phaophanit, who was shortlisted for the Turner Prize, and the founders of Brighton's Fabrica Gallery.[29]

Fabrica

In March 1996, the former Regency Holy Trinity Church in central Brighton was transformed into Fabrica, a visual arts organisation founded by a group of artists from Red Herring Studios. The church had closed the following year and was at first intended to be repurposed as a local history museum. When this did not happen, the Red Herring artists, supported by several organisations including South East Arts and Brighton Borough Council, were able to use the space to realise their vision of a

Fabrica Sign, 2019 by Evlynn Sharp.

"focus for contemporary visual art practice." Serving as one of the city's only major exhibition spaces for contemporary art, Fabrica commissions "art installations specific to the building" and their first exhibition took place in 1996.

To reflect the spirit of creation that they wanted to be the space's founding principle, the name Fabrica, which means "factory" in some European languages, was chosen for its etymological connections with the English "fabricate" and French *"fabriquer"*, meaning "to make". As well as offering a space and support for artists to create daring work, Fabrica encourages "an open dialogue between artists and visitors." They also endeavour to facilitate audience access, engagement and understanding of the showcased work through workshops, screenings and talks as part of "an integrated programme of education and audience development activity."[30]

ONCA

A belief in and commitment to art's power to bring about real socio-political change

underlies the highly innovative and unique work of O N C A. Based in a Grade II-listed Regency building in St George's Place, the gallery and performance space offers a platform for discussion, learning and artistic work tackling environmental and social issues, with the aim of inspiring positive action. O N C A's owner, Laura, was inspired to address these issues after meeting a puma named Wayra on a trip to Bolivia. She opened the organisation in 2012, taking its name from the Latin for jaguar.

O N C A's events programme is varied and impressive, featuring events curated both by the O N C A team and visiting artists and organisations, ranging from site-specific theatre to Synthetic Ecology.[31] As well as running workspaces for artists, charities and businesses,

Gallery front of O N C A, 2019 by Kavitha Ravikumar.

O N C A partners with local and international artists and organisations, with a focus on creative learning projects with children and young people.

Film

Brighton is a city with a rich cinematic history, frequently featuring as an iconic and distinctive film location:

> 'Several writers, most notably Steve Chibnall and Andy Medhurst, have analysed Brighton's repeated appearance in British films as a narrative terminus, an end-of-the-road/line/ pier location yielding either death and disillusion (*Brighton Rock* itself, of course; but also *Jigsaw, Villain, Quadrophenia, Mona Lisa, Dirty Weekend, London to Brighton*) or an uncorseted escape from mundane routine (*Penny Points to Paradise, Genevieve, Carry On at Your Convenience*).' [32]

The city has also long been home to alternative and independent cinemas. Some showed only old films and were known as "flea pits",[33] including The Gaiety and The Arcadia on Lewes Road.

Cinescene and Continentale

Cinescene and Continentale were run by Myles Byrne, a true creative eccentric – "the sort of character who belongs in a good comic novel." He balanced his role as Conservative councillor with managing theatres and cinemas along the south coast. He subsidised "art house" cinema at the Cinescene in North Street with "low-rent pornographic films at his one-time flagship, the Continentale in Kemptown."

Cinescene cinema by Dusashenka. From *Back Row Brighton*, 2009 QueenSpark Books.

Continentale cinema, past by Robert Jeeves, and present by Sue Craig. From *Back Row Brighton*, 2009 QueenSpark Books.

The Cinescene was variously re-named and re-branded over the years. It originally opened as the Bijou Electric Empire in 1911, becoming the Select Palace in 1918, before being renamed the Prince's and then the Myles Byrne Film Centre. Newsreels and cartoons were screened in "a small and slightly lopsided auditorium that had once been a printing works" until it became the Jacey in 1966, when "erotic" features were screened in an attempt to raise more revenue.

After three years as the Jacey, the premises were purchased by the British Film Institute and renamed the British Film Theatre, showcasing "art house" films. When BFI funding was withdrawn, Myles Byrne relaunched it as the Cinescene, keeping the "art house" style:

> ❛Filmgoers of a certain age will have fond memories of the somewhat deaf and doddery old couple who ran the front-of-house operations [at Cinescene]

> [...] alas, the quality of their tea and cakes was rarely equal to that of the films.❜

Sadly, the venue continued to lose money and eventually closed in 1983, having since been replaced by a "film-themed" Burger King. Alongside managing the Cinescene, Myles Byrne had been screening risqué, unusual and sometimes award-winning European films at the Continentale since the 1950s. It continued to show adult features until Byrne's death in 1986. A block of flats now stands on the Kemptown site.[34]

The Duke of York's

With its stripy legs extending from its roof and striking baroque architecture, the Duke of York's Picturehouse on the Preston Circus roundabout is a cultural landmark. Unsurprisingly, it features in *The Deckchair Guide to Brighton and Hove*'s top ten buildings in the city.[35] The Duke of York's was one of the UK's first purpose-built cinemas, opening in September 1910. It was constructed on the site of Henry Longhurst's

Prince's cinema, North Street, Brighton, c.1933.
Royal Pavilion & Museums.

Amber Ale Brewery, with the malthouse wall forming the auditorium's north wall. The first showing was *Byways of Byron*, made by pioneering local filmmaker George Albert Smith, who had a studio in St Anne's Well Gardens and later in Wilbury Villas.[36]

Although it is now part of the Picturehouse chain, the Duke of York's still shows predominantly art house films and has been home to the Cinecity festival of world cinema, which has taken place every November since 2003. The Duke of York's occupies a fond place in the memories of Brightonians:

'It was considered the height of luxury during its early years and its famous advertising slogan was "bring her to the duke's, it is fit for a duchess." The iconic black and white striped cancan legs that protrude from the cinema roof first appeared in 1991. The then owner, Bill Heine, had them made for another cinema he owned in Oxford called Not the Moulin Rouge. The legs are now an integral part of the Duke of York's advertising logo.' [37]

Duke of York's Cinema, c.2006 by Hassocks5489.

Duke of York's, c.1910. Royal Pavilion & Museums.

Many residents hold distinctive childhood memories of visits to the Duke of York's. Andy Steer recalls:

> ... eating chips on the way up New England Hill after our very first film in about 1954, *Shane* with Alan Ladd at the Duke of York's. The tingle of excitement as the little boy looked under the saloon doors at the end of the film, I can still conjure. [38]

John, who later became a projectionist at the cinema, remembers:

> ... watching *Zulu* (1964) there – they used to run continuous performances, and they didn't throw you out – you could come in in the middle of a film and watch it through, so you could see the end first. [39]

The Duke of York's was also Barbara Chapman's "first cinema":

> The films were shown in black and white, with no sound, only a piano being played. Laurel and Hardy and Charlie Chaplin films were my favourites and still make me laugh today. Charles Laughton left a vivid impression on me when I saw him in the film

Jamaica Inn, which in parts, I found rather frightening [...] When Charlie Chaplin's talking film *Modern Times* was to be shown, cinemas had to have new equipment installed to be able to hear and see this film, which everyone thought was marvellous.'[40]

The cinema still proves popular with youngsters today; Scout, aged 10, says:

'I usually go to the Duke of York's. I go there practically every Saturday morning with my dad at ten o'clock for Kids' Club and for the drawing competition. I've won twice! There's also a raffle. I haven't won that yet.'[41]

38A in Brighton, 2019 by Evlynn Sharp.

Notes

1 Will Rathbone, 'A Guide to Street Art in Brighton', *Culture Calling*, 31 July 2017.

2 Stuart Bagshaw and David Oates, *Brighton Graffiti* (London: Prestel, 2008).

3 *ZAP: Twenty-Five Years of Innovation*.

4 *Brighton Graffiti*.

5 Tim Lay, ed., *The Deckchair Guide to Brighton and Hove* (Brighton: QueenSpark Publishers, 2007).

6 'What we do', *Same Sky*.

7 Bex Bastable, 'Everything you need to know about Burning the Clocks in Brighton', *Brighton and Hove Independent*, 7 December 2018.

8 'Burning the Clocks', *Same Sky*.

9 Gerry Holloway and Frank Jackson, *Open House: A historical survey of the Fiveways Artists Group* (Brighton: More Than Ninety Minutes Publishing, 1999), p. 5.

10 Ibid.

11 Ibid.

12 Ibid.

13 Ibid.

14 Ibid.

15 Ibid.

16 Ibid.

17 Ibid.

18 Ibid.

19 Ibid.

20 Ibid.

21 Ibid.

22 *Artists' Open Houses*, 'About'.

23 *ZAP: Twenty-Five Years of Innovation*.

24 'About Us', *North Star Collective*.

25 Phoenix Brighton, 'Frequently Asked Questions about Phoenix'.

26 Ibid. 'About Us'.

27 Ibid. 'Frequently Asked Questions about Phoenix'.

28 Red Herring Studios, 'Who We Are'.

29 *Brighton and Hove Independent*, '"Gentrification" pushing creatives out of Brighton and Hove'.

30 Fabrica, 'About Us and Our History', *Fabrica: Brighton's Centre for Contemporary Art*.

31 O N C A, 'What We Do'.

32 Sarah Hutchings and John Riches, eds., *Back Row Brighton* (Brighton: QueenSpark Books, 2009).

33 Leila Abrahams, *Me and My Mum* (Brighton: QueenSpark Books, 1996).

34 *Back Row Brighton*.

35 *Deckchair Guide*, (Brighton: QueenSpark Books, 2007).

36 John Blackwell, 'A Potted History: Duke of York's Cinema'. My Brighton and Hove.

37 *Back Row Brighton*.

38 Andy Steer, *Brighton Boy* (Brighton: QueenSpark Books, 1994).

39 *Back Row Brighton*.

40 Barbara Chapman, *Boxing Day Baby* (Brighton: QueenSpark Books, 1994).

41 *Back Row Brighton*.

Afterword

Personal reflections from the writers and editors

'I first visited Brighton on a day trip at the age of 14 back in 1969. I knew after one day that this was the place I wanted to live; I came here as a student and have never felt the need to leave. I have travelled all over the world but as soon as I walk down Kensington Gardens I feel the spirit of Brighton; that unpredictable place where you can be who you want to be, wear what you feel like – it is the place to be.' GILL

'It has been such an exciting experience uncovering the many hidden and forgotten spaces and people that make up the alternative cultural patchwork of Brighton and Hove. Born and raised here myself, like many others I feel incredibly lucky to call such a creative, innovative and inclusive place home.' HANNAH

'I consider myself very lucky to have grown up in Brighton. I have come to appreciate this more since moving away to university and living abroad; across the world, this city is known as an interesting, vibrant and truly unique place. Researching and writing this book has definitely made me realise how fortunate I am to call this city my home. It was fascinating and inspiring to find out about the many talented, creative people of Brighton, both past and present, and the amazing things that they have done.' SIOBHÁN

When reading through the archives and other sources it became clear that there appears to be a "Brighton Effect". People come to Brighton and feel at home. The opportunity to delve into the QueenSpark archives and other local sources highlighted the variety of ways that alternative spaces have supported the development of the arts, people, culture and politics in Brighton. The information we found helped to create the different themes for the chapters. The following quote epitomises the spirit, creativity and innovation embodied by many of the organisations and people referred to in this book:

'While the city's reputation as home to a left leaning, socially aware, politically conscious population can sometimes feel a bit worn, on the whole it does seem true that if you want to change something yourself, Brighton & Hove is one of the more inspiring places to do it.'
TIM LAY, *THE DECKCHAIR GUIDE TO BRIGHTON AND HOVE*, QUEENSPARK BOOKS, 2007

Bibliography

Chapter 1: Writing and Reading

- Bartram, Dawn, Margaret Bearfield, Marion Devoy et al., *Stories from the Nights at the Round Table* (Brighton: QueenSpark Books, 1998)

- Cupidi, Richard, 'The Intrepid Bookseller of Brighton', https://unbound.com/boundless/2018/09/11/more-than-a-bookshop (Accessed: 14.'05, 22.'01.'19)

- Dennis, Peter, Beccie Mannall and Linda Pointing, *Daring Hearts* (Brighton: QueenSpark Books in collaboration with Brighton Ourstory, 1992)

- Olsen, Tillie, *Silences*

- Pitman, Barry, contributor

- QueenSpark Stroke Writing Group, *Life after Stroke* (Brighton: QueenSpark Books, 1993)

- QueenSpark Women Writers, *QueenSpark Women Writers* (Brighton: QueenSpark Books, 1984)

- QueenSpark Women Writers, *Writers Reign* (Brighton: QueenSpark Books, 1991)

- Shire, John, *Bookends: A Partial History of the Brighton Book Trade* (Brighton: Invocations Press, 2011)

- Woodham, Jonathan M., Neil Butler, Roger Ely et al., *ZAP: Twenty-Five Years of Innovation* (Brighton: QueenSpark Books, 2007)

- https://queensparkbooks.org.uk/about-2 (Accessed: 16.03, 22.01.19)

- https://www.kemptownbookshop.co.uk (Accessed: 14.15, 25.01.19)

- https://www.city-books.co.uk (Accessed: 14.17, 25.01.19)

Chapter 2: Political Spaces

- Carder, Timothy, *The Encyclopaedia of Brighton*

- Lakoff, George, *Moral Politics*

- Noyce, John and Francis Jarman (ed.), *Alternative Brighton*, 1973

- *The Mole* 1969

- https://blogs.brighton.ac.uk/radicalpress

- https://www.generalistarchive.co.uk

- https://blogs.brighton.ac.uk/radicalpress/category/title-librarians-for-social-change

- https://blogs.brighton.ac.uk/radicalpress/2016/08/21/david-mercer

- https://revealdigital.com/independent-voices

- https://unbound.com/boundless/2018/09/11/more-than-a-bookshop

Chapter 3: Music

- Batchelor, Marjory, *A Life Behind Bars* (Brighton: QueenSpark Books, 1999)

- Bailey, Ben, Richmond Bar: from jazz to punk 'The Richmond Returns', *The Brighton Source*, https://brightonsource.co.uk/news/the-richmond-returns (Accessed:13.'23, 03.'03.'19)

- Chapman, Barbara, *Boxing Day Baby* (Brighton: QueenSpark Books, 1994)

- Broadbent, Tim, 'Circus Circus, 2 Preston Road-previously Stanford Arms', *My Brighton and Hove*, http://www.mybrightonandhove.org.uk/page_id__6290_path__0p115p204p619p.aspx (Accessed: 12.'02, 22.'02.'19)

- Courtney, David, Allan Fowler, Damian Harris, James Kendall and The Perv, 'Brighton since the 60s', *The Brighton Source*, https://brightonsource.co.uk/features/live-brighton-since-the-60s (Accessed: 08.'50, 23.'01.'19)

- Dennis, Peter, Beccie Mannall and Linda Pointing, *Daring Hearts* (Brighton: QueenSpark Books in collaboration with Brighton Ourstory, 1992)

- Ditch, Gill, contributor

- Kitt, Jessica, 'From the "Mod" to the Modern: The Lowdown on Brighton's Music Scene', *Picture Britain*, http://www.picturebritain.com/2013/07/brightonmusic.html (Accessed: 07.'51, 24.'02.'19)

■ Noyce, John and Francis Jarman, *Alternative Brighton* (Brighton: Unicorn Bookshop Publications, 1973)

■ O'Loughlin, Terry, 'Regent Dance Hall', *My Brighton and Hove*, http://www.mybrightonandhove.org.uk/page_id__6373.aspx (Accessed: 13.'08, 03.'03.'19)

■ Ray, A. J., 'Siren Brunswick Performance Review', *Gscene*, November 2018

■ Siren, contributor

■ Various, *Blighty Brighton* (Brighton: QueenSpark Books, 1991)

■ Woodham, Jonathan M., 'The 'Art College' Basement: some recollections', University of Brighton, http://arts.brighton.ac.uk/arts/alumni-and-associates/the-history-of-arts-education-in-brighton/the-art-college-basement-some-recollections (Accessed 12.40, 12.02.19)

■ 'Remember the Regent', *Sparchives*, *Queen's Park News*, Spring '81

■ 'End of an era for "gatherers"', *The Argus*, 3 July 2000, https://www.theargus.co.uk/news/5161456.End_of_an_era_for__gatherers (Accessed: 13.28, 03.03.19)

■ 'London Road Station as an Asset', *The Round Hill Society*, http://www.roundhill.org.uk/main.php?sec=community&p=London_Road_Station_a_heritage_asset (Accessed 12.30, 12.02.19)

■ https://www.punkbrighton.co.uk/vaultn.html (Accessed 12.15, 12.02.19)

■ http://www.brightonourstory.co.uk/brighton-s-history/a-history-of-lesbian-and-gay-brighton-chapter-4-a-community-comes-of-age-1988-2001 (Accessed 12.02, 12.02.19)

Chapter 4: The Zap Club

■ Woodham, Jonathan M, Neil Butler, Roger Ely, Liz Agiss, Ian Smith, Simon Fanshawe, Sian Thomas, Richard Paul-Jones, Paul Kemp, Mark Waugh, Polly Marshall, Gavin Henderson, Paul Collard, Jane McMorrow, Dave Reeves, Rebecca Ball, Karen Poley, *ZAP: Twenty-Five Years of Innovation (*Brighton: QueenSpark Books, 2007)

■ Timeline link that highlights the development of Zap: https://www.mybrightonandhove.org.uk/topics/topicent/zap-25-years-of-cultural-innovation/zap-history/zap-25-years-of-cultural-innovation-13

Chapter 5: Festivals, Performance and Theatre

■ The Argus, 'Pete McCarthy and the alternative comedy boom of the Eighties: Goodbye to a genius', *The Argus*, 9 October 2004, https://www.theargus.co.uk/news/6710905.goodbye-to-a-genius

■ Barker, Howard, 'Grey Theatre', *Brighton Voice*, no. 6, 1973, QueenSpark Archives

■ Brighton Festival, 'Our History', https://brightonfestival.org/about/about_brighton_festival/our_history

■ Brighton Fringe, 'Brighton Fringe Info', https://www.brightonfringe.org/fringe-info

■ Brighton Fringe, 'The Warren', https://www.brightonfringe.org/whats-on/the-warren-36558

■ Brighton Little Theatre, 'Who We Are', *Brighton Little Theatre*, https://www.brightonlittletheatre.com/about-us-1

■ Brighton Open Air Theatre, 'History of BOAT', *Brighton Open Air Theatre*, https://www.brightonopenairtheatre.co.uk/about-boat/history-of-boat

■ Burnard, Philip, 'Brighton Little Theatre', My Brighton and Hove, http://www.mybrightonandhove.org.uk/page/the_original_brighton_little_theatre?path=0p115p884p

■ Comben, Andrew, 'Brighton Festival: 50 years of "a city on the edge"'

■ Coult, Tony: interview with Jenny Harris, 'Brighton Combination', *Unfinished Histories*

■ dreamthinkspeak, 'About', *dreamthinkspeak*, http://dreamthinkspeak.com/about

■ 'The Fine Art of Performance: Living Legacies of UK Art Schools' event, produced by Prof. Gavin Butt, Attenborough Centre for the Creative Arts, University of Sussex, 20/02/2019

■ Greig, Noël, 'Brighton Combination', *Unfinished Histories*

■ Hemmings, Jeff, 'Stomp – Interview 2015', *Brighton's Finest*, 9 January 2015 https://brightonsfinest.com/music/interviews/spotlight/luke-cresswell-stomp/2015

■ Holloway, Gerry, and Frank Jackson, *Open House: A historical survey of the Fiveways Artists Group*, (Brighton: More Than Ninety Minutes Publishing, 1999)

■ Komedia, 'History', https://www.komedia.co.uk/history

Latest Brighton, 'Stage: Brighton's New Venture Theatre is never shy of tackling classic theatre', *Latest Brighton*, September 12 2017, https://thelatest.co.uk/brighton/2017/09/12/stage-brightons-new-venture-theatre-never-shy-tackling-classic-theatre

The Marlborough Pub and Theatre, 'About Us', http://www.marlboroughtheatre.org.uk/venue-info/about-the-marlborough

'Pink Fringe', http://www.marlboroughtheatre.org.uk/venue-info/about-pink-fringe

My Brighton and Hove, 'Memories of the Siren Theatre Company', http://www.mybrightonandhove.org.uk/page_id__6043.aspx

The New Venture Theatre, 'About Us', https://www.newventure.org.uk/about-us/2-uncategorised/1-about-us

Otherplace, 'About', https://www.otherplacebrighton.co.uk/about

Stuckey, Andrew, 'Q&A with Anne-Marie Williams, Manager at Brighton Open Air Theatre', *Ticket Source*, 17 January 2019, https://www.ticketsource.co.uk/blog/qa-brighton-open-air-festival

'Brighton Combination', *Unfinished Histories*, https://www.unfinishedhistories.com/history/companies/brighton-combination

Wadsworth, Jo, 'Brighton Festival: 50 years of "a city on the edge"', *The Telegraph*, https://www.telegraph.co.uk/travel/festivals-and-events/brighton-festival-history

'What's On: Festival '79 Brighton July-21-28', *Brighton Voice*, July 1979, QueenSpark Archives

Woodham, J.M., N. Butler, R. Ely, L. Aggiss, I. Smith, S. Fanshawe, S. Thomas, et al., *ZAP: Twenty-Five Years of Innovation* (Brighton: QueenSpark Books, 2007)

Woodham, Jonathan M., 'The "Art College" Basement: some recollections', University of Brighton http://arts.brighton.ac.uk/arts/alumni-and-associates/the-history-of-arts-education-in-brighton/the-art-college-basement-some-recollections

Yes/No Productions, 'Yes/No: What we do', https://www.yesnoproductions.co.uk/index.html#content4-h

Chapter 6: Innovators

Anslow, Amy, and Ruth Anslow. 2019. *HISBE.* Accessed January 2019. https://hisbe.co.uk

Barr, Damian. 2013. *Maggie and Me.* London: Bloomsbury

Brighton Voice, July 1976

Carder, Tim. 1990. "Dr Richard Russell." My Brighton and Hove. Accessed January 18, 2019. http://www.mybrightonandhove.org.uk/page_id__8719.aspx?path=0p117p157p1660p

Coachwerks, https://coachwerks.org/coachwerkers

Drury, J. 2012. "Sake Dean Mahomed." My Brighton and Hove. October 24. Accessed January 18, 2019. http://www.mybrightonandhove.org.uk/page_id__11174.aspx

Drury, J. 2006. "Magnus Volk, Famous Inventor". My Brighton and Hove. August 27. Accessed February 1, 2019. http://www.mybrightonandhove.org.uk/page_id__7536.aspx?path=0p117p157p348p

Drury, J. 2012. "Do you remember the shop? " My Brighton and Hove. April 19. Accessed January 18, 2019. http://www.mybrightonandhove.org.uk/page_id__10967.aspx

Foods, Infinity. 2016. "Infinity Foods Story." *InfinityFoodsRetail.* Accessed January 18, 2019. https://infinityfoodsretail.coop/our-coop/our-story

Free University Brighton, https://freeuniversitybrighton.org/about

Loans, Start up. 2013. *Food and Drink Retail.* Accessed November 2018. https://www.startuploans.co.uk/success-stories/hisbe

Moorhouse, Ruth, and Chris Randall. 1994. *Her Story: The Life of Phoebe Hessel.* (Brighton: QueenSparkBooks)

Noyce, John, and Francis Jarman. 1973. "Alternative Brighton." *Radical Brighton.* June. Accessed January 18, 2019. https://cpb-eu-w2.wpmucdn.com/blogs.brighton.ac.uk/dist/5/2141/files/2016/05/Alternative-Brighton-take-1-1wz6ypq.pdf

The Bevy, https://www.thebevy.co.uk

The Big Lemon, https://thebiglemon.com

Chapter 7: Visual Culture

Abrahams, Leila, *Me and My Mum* (Brighton: QueenSpark Books, 1996)

'About', *Artists' Open Houses*, https://aoh.org.uk/about-us

Bagshaw, Stuart and David Oates, *Brighton Graffiti* (London: Prestel, 2008)

Bastable, Bex, 'Everything you need to know about Burning the Clocks in Brighton', *Brighton and Hove Independent*, 7 December 2018 https://www.brightonandhoveindependent.co.uk/whats-on/everything-you-need-to-know-about-burning-the-clocks-in-brighton-1-8732337

Blackwell, John, 'A Potted History: Duke of York's Cinema', My Brighton and Hove, http://www.mybrightonandhove.org.uk/page_id__5645.aspx

Brighton and Hove Independent, '"Gentrification" pushing creatives out of Brighton and Hove', *Brighton and Hove Independent*, https://www.brightonandhoveindependent.co.uk/news/gentrification-pushing-creatives-out-of-brighton-and-hove-1-7855807

Chapman, Barbara, *Boxing Day Baby* (Brighton: QueenSpark Books, 1994)

Fabrica, 'About Us and Our History', *Fabrica: Brighton's Centre for Contemporary Art*, https://www.fabrica.org.uk/about-us

Holloway, Gerry, and Frank Jackson, *Open House: A historical survey of the Fiveways Artists Group* (Brighton: More Than Ninety Minutes Publishing, 1999)

Hutchings, Sarah and John Riches, eds., *Back Row Brighton* (Brighton: QueenSpark Books, 2009)

Lay, Tim, ed., *The Deckchair Guide to Brighton and Hove* (Brighton: QueenSpark Publishers, 2007)

North Star Collective, 'About Us', *North Star Collective*, https://northstarstudio.wordpress.com/about

O N C A, 'What We Do', https://onca.org.uk/about/what-we-do

Phoenix Brighton, 'Frequently Asked Questions about Phoenix', *Phoenix Brighton*, https://www.phoenixbrighton.org/about-us

Rathbone, Will, 'A Guide to Street Art in Brighton', *Culture Calling*, 31 July 2017, https://www.culturecalling.com/features/a-guide-to-street-art-in-brighton

'Who We Are', *Red Herring Studios*, https://www.redherringstudios.org/history

'What we do', *Same Sky*, http://samesky.co.uk/what-we-do. 'Burning the Clocks', http://samesky.co.uk/events/burning-the-clocks

Sheerin, Mark, 'Phoenix Brighton reveals ambitious plans for £2.5m south coast arts centre', *Culture24*, 17 March 2010, https://www.culture24.org.uk/art/art77150

Steer, Andy, *Brighton Boy* (Brighton: QueenSpark Books, 1994)

Woodham, Jonathan M., 'The "Art College" Basement: some recollections', University of Brighton, http://arts.brighton.ac.uk/arts/alumni-and-associates/the-history-of-arts-education-in-brighton/the-art-college-basement-some-recollections

Woodham, J.M., N. Butler, R. Ely, L. Aggiss, I. Smith, S. Fanshawe, S. Thomas, et al., *ZAP: Twenty-Five Years of Innovation* (Brighton: QueenSpark Books, 2007).

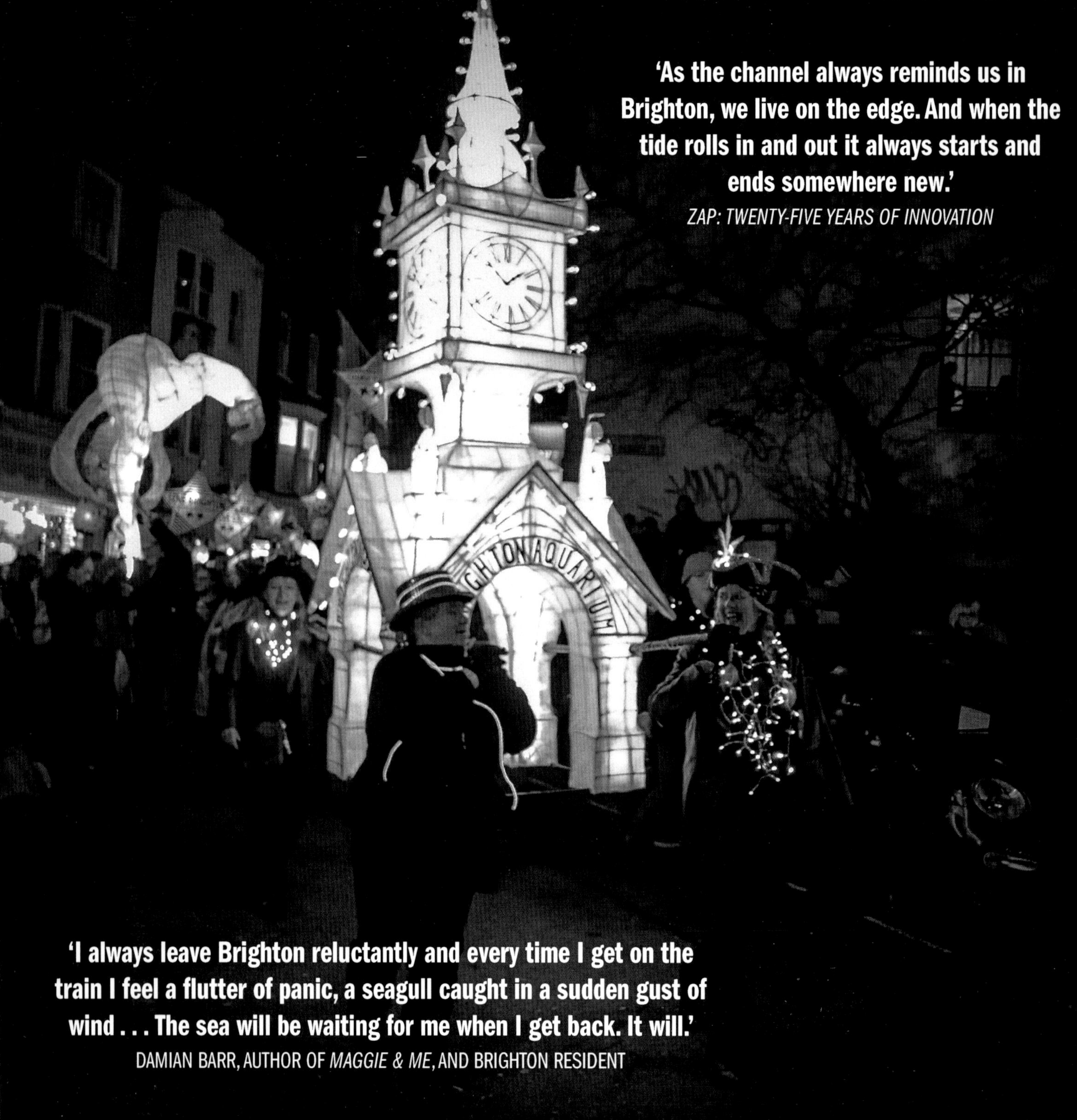

'As the channel always reminds us in Brighton, we live on the edge. And when the tide rolls in and out it always starts and ends somewhere new.'
ZAP: TWENTY-FIVE YEARS OF INNOVATION

'I always leave Brighton reluctantly and every time I get on the train I feel a flutter of panic, a seagull caught in a sudden gust of wind . . . The sea will be waiting for me when I get back. It will.'
DAMIAN BARR, AUTHOR OF MAGGIE & ME, AND BRIGHTON RESIDENT